dis·course in·to·na·tion

A Discourse-Pragmatic Approach to Teaching the Pronunciation of English

LUCY PICKERING

Texas A & M–Commerce

University of Michigan Press
Ann Arbor

ISBN-13: 978-0-472-03018-7

2021   2020   2019   2018   4   3   2   1

To Jean & Jack Pickering, for all of it.

ACKNOWLEDGMENTS

My sincere thanks go to Kelly Sippell, the most gracious and professional of editors, who has done much to improve this manuscript as it has developed. This book was conceived during a conversation with Ann Wennerstrom whose support, both professionally and personally, I cherish. I owe a considerable intellectual debt to the work of both John Gumperz and David Brazil. Although I never had the opportunity to meet David, I have been able to "channel" him through Richard Cauldwell, who has in turn had a significant impact on my thinking, and who has also become a dear friend. To Andrea Tyler, Diana Boxer, and Caroline Wiltshire, under whose tutelage my work in discourse intonation began—thank you for trusting me to do the work. Without your support, it would not have been possible to get here.

I also acknowledge and thank all the participants of my research whose willingness to be studied and recorded has made this work possible, and the students in my Applied Phonology classes in Alabama, Washington (DC), Georgia, and Texas who have helped me shape the material during their reading of previous drafts. Many thanks to my TAs in Texas, Meichan Huang and Shigehito Menjo, who helped with the final phases, and to my colleague Mark Haslett from KETR Radio, who generously opened his studio and worked with me recording the sound files for the book.

I am delighted to have the opportunity to include the work of Colleen Meyers and Catherine and Mark DeGaytan in the book and very thankful that they agreed to attach themselves to the project. To the numerous other colleagues, family, and friends who have supported me in this project—thank you.

I sat in a number of different home offices as I completed this work but was always surrounded by dogs patiently waiting for walks or food. Thank you Misha, Bailey, Boo, Chloe, Tempest, and Blue for keeping me company and giving me something else to think about, even if it is giant holes in the yard.

This book also belongs to my husband, Salvatore Attardo, whose "book boot camp" marked the beginning of the last leg home and who is my best coach, my best reader, and my best everything else besides.

CONTENTS

INTRODUCTION

I suspect that if you ask a group of ESL/EFL teachers to recall their training in phonology, or the sound system of English, you would find few of them who remember specific instruction in the area of English intonation. Most of what we know, we have picked up along the way. We find we have collected an ad hoc assortment of rules related to grammatical categories and a host of ill-defined patterns that we believe express certain attitudes or emotions. It is little wonder that many teachers and teacher trainers, while recognizing that intonation is crucial for communicative competence, approach this area of language development with a sense of unease, if at all.

The purpose of this book is to provide an accessible introduction to **discourse intonation** for ESL/EFL teachers. The originator of the discourse-pragmatic model presented here, David Brazil, was first and foremost a teacher. He was recruited as a researcher at the University of Birmingham, U.K., to work with a group of discourse analysts. During that time, he wrote a number of research papers and several manuscripts, including *The Communicative Value of Intonation in English* (1985/1997), which forms the basis for the description of the model presented in this book. In addition, he conducted a number of workshops for the British Council in which he focused on the pedagogical applications of the model.

Although we are in an era of excellent English language training books for teachers, intonation has remained what Wrembel (2007, p. 189) refers to as the "problem child" from a pedagogical perspective. The reasons for learners' difficulties in this area have been discussed in the literature for some time (Clennell, 1997), and they continue to be reiterated today. Some of the reasons include: the need for a focus on the pragmatic function of intonation (Reed & Michaud, 2015), more innovation in teaching materials (Pickering, 2004), and a lack of confidence and training in this area that handicaps teachers in the classroom (Foote, Holtby, & Derwing, 2012; Macdonald, 2002). Yet, as Mennen (2007) notes, we cannot afford to neglect the teaching and learning of intonation in the L2 classroom if we wish to give our learners every chance of success:

> Given that we derive much of our impressions about a speaker's attitude and disposition toward us from the way they use intonation in speech, listeners may form a negative impression of a speaker based on the constantly inappropriate use of intonation. (p. 54)

Therefore, this text is a practical introduction to teaching intonation using Brazil's model. The chapters are organized to familiarize readers with the different parts of the model and the ways they can be used effectively in the classroom to teach this important linguistic system. Chapters 2–5 describe the four systems that make up the model: tone unit structure, prominence, tone choice, and key and termination choice. Chapter 6 focuses in more detail on speakers' choices of tone, particularly in asymmetrical interactions in which there is some kind of power differential, such as that between teacher and student. Chapters 7 and 8 then examine how discourse intonation choices impact cross-cultural interaction, particularly between speakers of different Englishes—that is, between speakers of General American English, for example, and those of New Englishes such as Indian English or those in an English as a lingua franca context. Chapter 9 examines evidence regarding the teachability and learnabilty of intonation, and Chapter 10 concludes the presentation.

Important terms and concepts are boldfaced and appear in the glossary. All chapters include a Check Your Learning section and activities for discussion or that are hands-on. Chapters 3–9 also include sections specifically focused on implications for instruction. Examples that have corresponding sound files are identified by the ear icon and the number of the file (e.g., SF 2.1, 2.2) and are available at www.press.umich.edu/elt/compsite/DI.

Preliminaries

This book assumes that readers have taken an Introduction to Linguistics course or have some basic familiarity with the concepts that would be covered in such a course, particularly as they relate to the intonation system of English. That said, pronunciation textbooks often vary in the particular terms they use. For example, the term **intonation** is narrowly defined in English as the use of pitch structure over the length of a given utterance. It can also be defined more broadly as concerning not only pitch structure but also rhythm and stress patterns. This corresponds to the definition of **suprasegmentals,** which contrasts with **segmentals** and refers more generally to **pitch,** stress, volume, and pause patterns (see Figure I.1). This book also uses the term **prosody,** or **prosodic system,** interchangeably with both **intonation** and **suprasegmentals** to reflect this broader focus.

Readers may also not be familiar with the term **discourse-pragmatic** as it is used here. It defines an approach to the intonation system in English that focuses on its role in <u>text structure</u>, as opposed to sentence structure, and describes the intonation choices that speakers make as conventionalized responses to the specific <u>linguistic</u> and <u>social contexts</u> of a given interaction.

In addition to these definitions, several foundational concepts are briefly outlined to provide a framework for what will follow. It will undoubtedly be the case that some readers will be more familiar with some of these concepts than others.

Intonation as a Grammatical System

Intonation in any given language or dialect has two important characteristics: First, it operates within a standard set of conventions or recognized norms that are shared between speaker-hearers of that language or dialect; and second, speaker-hearers within that speech community have unconscious (or tacit) knowledge of those conventions even if they are unable to verbalize them consciously. Let's briefly consider another linguistic system—syntax (sentence structure)—as an example of a grammatical system. If we are competent speakers of English, we know that a grammatical sentence has a specified order of components and that certain elements of the sentence appear before others— for example, *a white dog* vs. **dog white a*. In addition, we may also know the English language rule or convention that applies here, which is that of a well-formed noun phrase: an article (*a*) is followed by an adjective (*white*), which is followed by a noun (*dog*) as opposed to, for example, a well-formed sentence of French, in which a different noun phrase order applies. Regardless of whether an English speaker can verbalize this rule consciously, (s)he understands tacitly that **dog white a* is an ungrammatical sentence.

Intonation is the grammatical system that includes our use of pitch, pause, and **prominence** (or sentence stress) and is a sub-field of the phonological system of a language. The sub-field is called **suprasegmentals,** or **prosody,** and its place in the sound system (or phonology) of English is highlighted in Figure I.1.

The conventions that apply to this linguistic system address how we group our words together in prosodic units, how we understand turn-taking cues in conversation, and how we assess if someone might be signaling to us that they are feeling angry or sad. However, there are complications that arise when we try

Figure I.1. Sound System of English

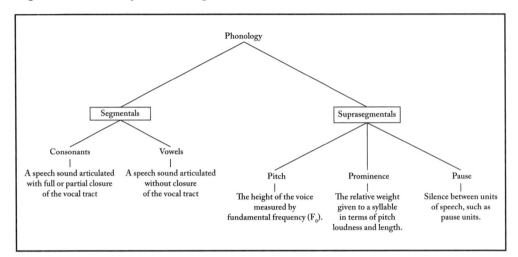

to describe this system. First, as we said, these conventions are usually entirely tacit. Competent speakers will follow these norms but may find it impossible to consciously recreate the specific intonational cues or signals that are being used. For example, we may recognize when a speaker sounds odd or strange but find it difficult to "unpack" the reasons for our perception, particularly with regard to pitch.

Second, unlike syntax, whose units of description (verbs, nouns, adjectives, and so on) we inherited from Greek and Latin scholars and which have remained essentially unchanged for hundreds of years, descriptions of intonation have been far less uniform. Historically, there has been far less agreement as to both (1) how best to describe the building blocks that make up the system and (2) how exactly intonation interacts with other linguistic systems such as syntax and semantics to signal conventional meanings to speakers. This book presents one system, Brazil's Discourse Intonation, which has been used successfully in English language classrooms for the last 25 years and appears in currently available textbooks by Cauldwell (2013) and Gorsuch et al. (2010).

Pragmatic Approaches to Intonation

It is axiomatic to say that we use language to communicate with each other. However, when we think carefully about how that communication takes place effectively, we find that it relies on some assumptions that are so implicit that we rarely think about them. When we engage in normal interaction with another speaker-hearer, we assume that they are designing their conversational contribution to be as cooperative as possible and encourage successful communication. This means that we come to a given speech event assuming that the person we are addressing is both following the norms or conventions that we would expect and expressing them in the way we would expect. In communication with speaker-hearers from outside our speech community, however, both these assumptions may be incorrect. Let's look at the example of turn-taking conventions in conversation.

In General American English (GAE), there is a norm in conversation referred to as "the no gap, no overlap" rule. If one speaker finishes a turn and two speakers then begin to speak at the same time, one will yield to the other. Any long gap between turns or considerable overlap between speakers is dispreferred (Sacks, Schlegloff, & Jefferson, 1974). This does not hold for all speech communities, however. Reisman (1974) describes his experience in a Lapp (or Saami) community in northern Sweden where long "conversational gaps" were the norm:

> We spent some days in a borrowed sod house in the village of Rensjoen . . . . Our neighbors would drop in on us every morning just to check that things were all right. We would offer coffee. After several minutes of silence the offer would be accepted. We would tentatively ask a question. More silence, then a 'yes' or a 'no'. Then a long wait. After five or ten minutes we would ask another. Same pause, same 'yes' or 'no'. Another ten minutes, etc. Each visit lasted approximately an hour . . . . During that time there would be six or seven exchanges. Then our guests would leave to repeat the performance the next day. (pp. 112–113)

Such differences in conventions can also been seen across varieties or dialects within languages. Within General American English, Tannen (1981) talks about the opposite situation of the Sweden example in her discussion of "machine gun questions" used by the New Yorkers in her dinner party data. These are described as questions uttered quickly and overlapping or "latching" immediately onto someone else's turn, which made the non–New Yorker participants feel interrupted, rushed, or otherwise uncomfortable.

The importance of establishing cooperation and rapport-building between interlocutors and how that can be expressed differently (but systematically) between speech communities is an excellent example of the pragmatic importance of intonation. In GAE, there are systematic intonational cues or signals used by the speaker and understood by the hearer to indicate a range of communicative functions, including highlighting information (see Chapter 3), indicating [dis]agreement, or expressing social distance (see Chapter 6). As none of us speaks in a monotone, pitch movements will always be present, and hearers will always interpret them. When communication crosses speech communities, such cues can be easily misunderstood.

Intonational Variation in Varieties of English

English is a global language comprised not of one monolithic variety but of many different ones. We are used to hearing systematic differences in the lexical, syntactic, and phonological features (including intonational ones) of different dialects within one variety (such as Southern U.S. English vs. General American English) and different traditional varieties (such as British English vs. Canadian English). However, most of us are less familiar with the systematic differences that occur in Indian English or African English, and even further, with the potential systematic features in interactions between speakers of **English as a Lingua Franca (ELF).** From a historical perspective, we can trace the development of different continental varieties of English through "dispersals or diasporas" (Jenkins, 2009, p. 5). The first dispersal came with the migration of U.K. immigrants to the new world, namely the United States, Canada, Australia, and New Zealand. The second was the result of colonization in Asia and Africa. We can also think of the growing number of speakers of English as a foreign language (EFL) across much of the rest of the world as an additional dispersal of English as a Lingua Franca.

In the field of World Englishes, this division has been codified by Kachru (1985). The model comprises three major groups of English: Inner Circle Englishes (varieties of English resulting from the first diaspora); Outer Circle Englishes (varieties of English resulting from the second diaspora); and Expanding Circle Englishes (varieties of English used in territories where English was taught as a foreign language and is increasingly the lingua franca). Although these categories are not unproblematic (see Jenkins 2009 for an excellent discussion), for the purposes of this volume, I retain the overall structure proposed by Kachru. I have, however, chosen to label them **Traditional Englishes** (i.e., first diaspora varieties such as U.S., Australian, and Canadian Englishes), **New Englishes** (i.e., second diaspora varieties such as African and Indian Englishes), and **Emerging Englishes** (i.e., sometimes described as Global Englishes in a Lingua Franca context). I have chosen these terms in order to avoid any negative associations that have become connected with Kachru's original terms over time. Although Kachru did not intend any notion of superiority to be inherent in his use of the term *inner circle*, the label casts a long shadow for both teachers and students in the English teaching profession with its strongly implied "gate keeping" function (Higgins, 2003). The term *traditional Englishes* adequately reflects the historical weight from which these varieties continue to derive their heft in most teaching contexts, without countenancing their historical privilege. Both new Englishes or *new varieties of English* (Kandiah, 1998) and *emerging Englishes* (Deterding & Kirkpatrick, 2006) are also more neutral terms to describe additional varieties that have often been disenfranchised in the past. The audio recordings accompanying this book reflect these multiple varieties and include examples from speakers of U.S. English, U.K. English, Indian English, and ELF.

A Final Note

The primary focus of this text is to lay down an approach to intonation that can be applied in an ESL/EFL context; a secondary goal is to demystify a linguistic sub-system that has often been marginalized or considered too variable to describe in the same way as we would other sub-systems in language such as syntax and morphology. Because of our unfamiliarity with intonational structures in language, it can be all too easy to get lost going down the theoretical garden path and decide that this is not an area that, as teachers or students, we are comfortable including in our classrooms. It is certainly true that there may be some initial "front end" work as we learn to navigate the system; however, I hope that this text will demonstrate that this is both an approachable and fruitful task.

Chart of Transcription Symbols

// //	Unit boundaries
CAPS	Prominence
UNDERLINE	Tonic syllable
High key	⇧
Mid key	⇨
Low key	⇩
Rising tones	↗ (r+); ↘↗ (r)
Falling tones	↘ (p); ↗↘(p+)
Level tone	→ (o)

Chapter 1

The Intonation System of English

"It's dreadful what little things lead people to misunderstand each other."
—*L.M. Montgomery*

1.1. Why Does Intonation Matter?

Let's start with an example from the world of work that we will come back to in Chapter 7. In the U.K., the largest minority group of citizens are from the Indian subcontinent. Many have learned at least some English in India; however, this variety (Indian English) is a **New English** that in some cases follows quite different conventions or norms from Standard British English. In an example focusing on intonational conventions, Gumperz (1982) describes how the unexpected intonation patterns of Indian and Pakistani English-speaking workers in a workplace cafeteria in Britain caused them to be perceived as uncooperative by their British English–speaking addressees. The incidents occurred in a cafeteria in a British airport in which Indian and Pakistani women were serving meals to a British English–speaking population of supervisors and cargo handlers who perceived them as "surly and uncooperative." When their interactions at the cafeteria were observed, it was clear that different conventional uses of rising and falling intonation patterns were at the core of the misunderstanding. For example, to ask a cargo handler if he wanted gravy with his meat, a British

English–speaking worker would say "↗Gravy?" using rising intonation, whereas an Indian English speaker would say "↘Gravy" using a falling intonation. This was interpreted as a demand from the worker rather than an offer and was perceived by the British English speakers as rude. Gumperz reported:

> When the Indian women heard this [intonation patterns], they began to understand the reactions they had been getting all along which had until then seemed incomprehensible. They then spontaneously recalled intonation patterns which had seemed strange to them when spoken by native English speakers. At the same time, supervisors learned that the Indian women's falling intonation was their normal way of asking questions in that situation, and that no rudeness or indifference was intended. (p. 173)

Gumperz goes on to report that once these conventions were discussed in the community, real improvements transpired in the interethnic communication that was common in this particular workplace. It seems unlikely, however, that this resolution would have occurred without an intervention and far more likely that racial discrimination (which the Indian workers initially felt was entirely to blame) would have become the sole culprit.

This example highlights two critical aspects of intonation systems in natural language. First, forms and functions are not universal across languages or even dialects of the same language; while some universals may exist (see Chapter 8 for more discussion), languages may use entirely different intonational structures to signal similar pragmatic messages. Second, as competent users of the language, we are not necessarily very good at reflecting on what intonation is and how we might use it. This is in part because we are unable to verbalize the conventions that underlie our intonation use; thus, when they are broken, the result is often interpreted as something outside the language system such as speaker attitude or bias. It is also in part because these linguistic behaviors become very powerful in transient events like speech where we have no time to reflect on why particular feelings might be triggered. In this sense, as Rubin (2011) notes, pronunciation can play a powerful role in **impression management**:

> Pronunciation is not merely acoustics; it has an active social life. Linguistic stereotyping is a robust mechanism of social judgment whereby listeners ascribe a myriad of traits to speakers based often on only very thin samples of pronunciation. (p. 16)

The next section traces in broad strokes the historical arc of the development of intonational models in English. The intent is to provide a brief background for the reader as a basis for understanding how current descriptions have emerged and why certain pedagogical traditions have developed. We begin with the division between British and American approaches to intonation and close with the most recent models that prioritize intonation in discourse.

1.2. Historical Approaches to Intonation

The history of English intonation analysis is commonly divided into two broad categories: the British tradition and the North American tradition. The first major study in British English was published by Steele in 1775, who was also the first to provide a systematic method of transcription—a very detailed musical notation in which he indicated pitch changes of a quarter and even an eighth of a tone. Probably the most influential early modern phonetician was Henry Sweet (1890), whose **tonal analysis** became the basis for much of the later work in the British tradition. Sweet identified five tones: three single tones (level, rise, and fall) and two compound tones (rise-fall and fall-rise), which were given attitudinal labels. A **rising tone,** for instance, could vary from indicating "an expectant or suspensive attitude" to signaling "a character of cheerfulness or geniality."

In 1922, Palmer posited that the tone group was the unit within which the five tones functioned. The **tone group** was a series of words containing one major stress (or **prominence**), which was divided into three segments: the **nucleus** (the stressed syllable), the **head**, which comprised anything before the nucleus, and the **tail**, which included anything after it. Although, over time, researchers have disagreed on the internal structure of the tone unit, the basic concept of the tone group continues to be the unit of analysis in most British intonation work up to the present day including in the model presented in this book.

Several years after Palmer's work was published, another influential yet very different method of analysis was suggested by Armstrong and Ward (1926) called **contour analysis.** They put forth the idea that two basic tunes can be described in terms of general grammatical categories and with a limited number of variations. Tune 1 is a falling tone used in expressions of certainty, while Tune 2 is a rising tune signaling uncertainty or incompleteness. Their transcription method, developed for the benefit of English language learners, consisted of simple contours made up of dots and dashes representing stressed and unstressed syllables. For the next few decades, researchers continued to work in either contour analysis or tone group analysis and described tone choice in terms of both grammatical categories and attitudinal characteristics. This type of **semantic labeling** reached its peak with O'Connor and Arnold (1961/1973), who created nearly 300 attitudinal categories in their taxonomy of tunes.

The most significant and long-lasting contribution to the British tradition at this time was made by Halliday (1967), who included an analysis of intonation as part of his framework of systemic grammar. Halliday believed that intonational contrasts were grammatical in nature. He stated that "we cannot fully describe the grammar of English without reference to the contrasts expounded by intonation" (p. 169). He was primarily concerned with **information struc-ture** and the function of intonation to mark information as given (old) or new. This model comprises three separate systems: tonality (tone unit divisions), tonicity (the internal structure of the unit), and tone (pitch movement on the final tonic syllable.) The final tonic syllable bears the information focus and is characterized by a rising (indicating uncertainty) or falling (indicating certainty) movement. An additional system identifies three pitch levels whose function is to describe **affective meaning**. Patterns are labeled with adjectival glosses such as "forceful or querulous" and "awestruck or disappointed" (1970, pp. 32–33). Halliday's analysis remains one the few attempts to completely integrate intonation into the grammatical system of English (Halliday & Greaves, 2008).

As the traditions of tonal and tune analyses were being developed and refined in Britain, a much different tradition was evolving on the other side of the Atlantic. The study of linguistics in North America was initially driven by Boas, Sapir, and Bloomfield (Robins, 1967), and the views of the latter two scholars regarding intonation prepared the way for much of its future treatment by American researchers. On the one hand, Sapir (1921) viewed intonation as a peripheral element outside of "pure" language: "All that part of speech which falls outside the rigid articulatory framework is not speech in idea, but is merely superadded, more or less instinctively determined vocal complication insepa-rable from speech in practice (note 2, p. 46)."

On the other hand, Bloomfield (1933) developed principles of **phonemic analysis** that extended into every level of linguistic structure, and intonation was no exception. He regarded intonation and stress as secondary phonemes, both because they could not be attached to a particular segment and because he regarded intonation as a way to modify speech. Although he developed five pitch and three stress phonemes, he continued to be ambiguous regarding their precise status:

> We use features of pitch very largely in the manner of gestures, as when we talk harshly, sneeringly, petulantly, caressingly, cheerfully and so on. In English, and in the languages of Europe generally, pitch is the acoustic feature where gesture-like variations, non-distinctive but socially effective, border most closely upon genuine linguistic distinctions. (p. 114)

Much of the work that directly followed Bloomfield was concerned with cementing the status of stress and intonation as distinctive linguistic features. The most thorough description at this time was given by Pike (1945), whose comprehensive phonemic treatment of intonation, stress, and pause and the accompanying transcription methods assured prosodic features a permanent place in mainstream linguistics. Pike posited four relative but significant levels of pitch, or pitch phonemes, as the basic building blocks for intonation contours. These are shown as a series of connected numbers representing the particular levels, such as 2-4 or 1-3. In addition to levels and contours, Pike identified two pause phonemes: tentative and final. The tentative pause tends to occur in places where the attitude of the speaker includes uncertainty or non-finality, and the final pause occurs when the speaker's attitude is one of completion. For Pike, intonation was strictly **attitudinal**:

> In English, then, an INTONATION MEANING modifies the lexical meaning of a sentence by adding to it the SPEAKER'S ATTITUDE towards the contents of that sentence . . . . These attitudes vary from surprise, to deliberation, to sharp isolation of some part of a sentence for attention, to mild intellectual detachment (pp. 21–23). (capitalization in original)

Pike listed approximately 30 primary contours and a number of modifications variously labeled in attitudinal terms such as "endearment," "detachedness," "mild attention," "incomplete deliberation," and so on. Pike's analysis was very influential, and the concept of four pitch phonemes and two juncture types became the norm. The strongest critic of this kind of analysis was another American, Dwight Bolinger. In his view, intonation was not phonemic: "The basic entity of intonation is the pattern, not a pattern in the relatively abstract sense of grammatical recurrences, but in the fundamental, down-to-earth sense of a continuous line that can be traced on a piece of paper (1951, p. 206)."

Not long after this debate however, the rise of **generative grammar,** which focused on creating a system of rules for interpreting sentence structure, consigned intonation to the edge of the field in most mainstream American linguistics. For example, intonation is purposely omitted from Chomsky and Halle's (1968) generative text *The Sound Pattern of English,* which refers readers to Stockwell (1964) and Lieberman (1966) who were attempting to generate intonation contours via transformational rules. This research was clearly problematic as there was no way to incorporate the attitudinal function of intonation into transformations. In order to deal with this issue, the researchers attempted to separate out the linguistic and non-linguistic aspects of intonation and, once again, the status of intonation as a linguistic system was called into question:

> The emotion of the speaker can modify the intonation of an utterance just as it can modify other aspects of the speech signal. . . . However, these aspects of intonation are not primary linguistic phenomena. They are apparently superimposed on the linguistically predictable aspects of intonation, though it is, at present, not clear how they are manifested in the acoustic signal. However, the effects of emotion are independent of the linguistic aspects of the speech signal. (Lieberman, 1966, p. 121)

To summarize, by the early 1970s, two distinct traditions in English intonation analysis had emerged. The British tradition was often criticized for a lack of a theoretical basis and an oversimplification of description, primarily for pedagogical purposes. The American system, on the other hand, had a strong theoretical bias, but perhaps one that was not entirely suited to the nature of prosodic phenomena as there was a tendency to characterize as extra-linguistic those features that did not fit neatly into the system.

1.3. Intonation in Discourse

As theoretical interest in linguistics shifted toward analysis of discourse throughout the 1970s and to the present day, intonation became less marginalized. Linguists such as Labov (1972) and Gumperz and Hymes (1972) who were working with natural speech and conversational analysis included it as an important aspect of spoken language that had an essential role in regulating interaction. Increasingly, discourse-based models recognized a multi-functional role for intonation, which is described by Chun (2002) and summarized as:

1. **Grammatical function** encompasses a number of primarily structural functions including the use of a final rising or falling pitch to distinguish utterances as statements or questions, and the employment of tone unit and pause structure to disambiguate relative clauses.

2. **Attitudinal function** comprises much of the work on the affective function of intonation that we have seen develop over the history of intonational analysis (previously described). However, recent models have moved away from too many precise labels and unnecessary complications as it is now widely recognized that affective meaning is communicated by a cluster of variables that include loudness, stress, rate, kinesics, and contextual expectation, among others.

3. **Discourse function** encompasses both informational and interactional aspects of pitch and pause structure. Studies have shown that systematic pitch and pause characteristics are linked to topic structure at both the local (utterance) and global (discourse) levels. Speakers use these features to mark boundary strength (e.g., an utterance boundary versus a paragraph boundary), and listeners use this information to parse information structure and predict upcoming information. Interactional functions of intonation include the use of pitch variation to regulate turn-taking in conversation, to communicate sociolinguistic information such as status differences, and to contribute to relationship-building between participants.

4. **Indexical function** describes the ways in which particular intonation patterns can mark a speaker's affiliation with a regional or sociocultural group. One example frequently discussed in both the linguistic and mainstream press is the high-rising terminal tone that marks a social dialect often referred to as Valley Girl, Mallspeak, or Uptalk.

A focus on patterns of intonation in discourse in conjunction with rapid developments in **digital speech processing** and synthesized speech have led to an increased interest in the role that intonation plays in natural interaction. The most recent model-building in intonation applies this discourse-pragmatic perspective, prioritizing the communicative value of the intonation system and continues to reveal the historical divide between British and American traditions. This can be shown using two different yet comprehensive frameworks developed by David Brazil (1985) and Janet Pierrehumbert (1980); each of which evolved with different purposes in mind: Brazil's model closely follows the British **functionalist tradition** and prioritizes the description of naturally occurring discourse. His concerns are both to understand the role of intonation in communication and develop a model that can be used as a basis for teaching English intonation to language learners. Pierrehumbert, on the other hand, follows the American generative tradition and builds a theoretical model of intonational phonology using language examples largely created and tested in the laboratory; applications of this model have included work in synthesized speech. Despite these very different orientations, where both models address the pragmatic function of intonation in discourse, they reach similar conclusions, as will be discussed in Chapter 2.

1.4. Pedagogical Impact of the Study of Intonation

This final section briefly examines the link between the historical development of intonation models and pedagogical practice as reflected in ESL/EFL textbooks spanning the past 50 years or so. The focus on the attitudinal or expressive function of intonation developed by O'Connor and Arnold (1961) reached its peak in O'Connor's *Better English Pronunciation*, first published in 1967 and currently still available in its second edition, published in 1980. In O'Connor's book (p. 121), intonation patterns are marked using diacritics to indicate types of attitude. For example, the "glide-up" is associated with a "soothing" or "encouraging" attitude:

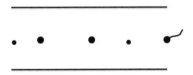

I won't drive too fast (so don't worry)

Whereas the "take-off" is associated with a "grumble":

I didn't hurt you (so why make all that fuss)

Pedagogical materials in the United States followed the pitch and juncture phonemic approach developed by Pike (1945) that accessed intonation through grammatical structure. There are four levels of significant pitch level choices that are numbered as: 4 = extra high; 3= high; 2 = middle; and 1= low. Students are introduced to common intonation patterns such as the declarative and interrogative patterns as numbered contours:

Declarative 2-3-1 Pattern

```
3 _____⌒
2 I CAN'T find the CAT\
1                      \
```

Interrogative 2-1-3 Pattern

```
3 _____/
2 Is the CAT in HERE?
1          \  /
            \/
```

The pedagogical tradition that is established in these materials can still be discerned in current popular texts for teachers. One very commonly used reference text in the United States for example, *Teaching Pronunciation* (Celce-Murcia et al., 2010) uses grammatical and attitudinal function as a means of understanding the intonation system, and retains among other concepts the declarative versus interrogative distinction and the transcription-level system.

As Levis (2016) notes, the field continues to struggle with how to combine current intonation research most productively with pedagogical materials:

> Since the late 1970s, theoretical and laboratory research into intonation has exploded with new findings, not only for English but for many other languages (e.g., Hirst & Di Cristo, 1998). Almost none of this research has found its way into teaching materials . . . textbooks still overemphasize intonation as a reflection of grammatical form and as having a special role in expressing emotional meaning, a belief that has long been questioned. (p. 427)

1.5. Summary

This chapter focused broadly on the importance of two approaches to the intonation system in English: structural and functional. This overview was not designed to be a comprehensive treatment of the historical development of intonation models in English. Detailed treatments can be found in several excellent texts including Cruttenden (1997) and Ladd (1996). The chapter briefly addressed some of the pedagogical applications of these models as they have appeared over time in ESL/EFL teaching practice. Chapter 2 will introduce a model of intonation based on a discourse-pragmatic perspective (Brazil, 1985/1997) and will discuss the ways in which it can form the basis for a more effective pedagogical model.

1.6. Check Your Learning

1. Why is studying/understanding intonation important?

2. What are the main differences between the British and American approaches to intonation?

3. How would you briefly describe the history of ESL/EFL textbooks' approach to teaching intonation?

1.7. Activities

1. The phonetician Daniel Jones (1881–1967) was almost certainly the inspiration for Professor Higgins in George Bernard Shaw's play *Pygmalion*, which was adapted into the film *My Fair Lady* (1964). In the movie, Professor Higgins uses a xylophone to teach his student how to change her intonation, which he perceives as very flat. In 2005, Rebecca Hincks developed a measure of pitch variation that can be used to detect the perceived "liveliness" of second language learner speech (Hincks, 2005). Discuss your experience as a teacher and/or learner of English working with the intonation system. What is your perception of your learners' speech? Does it seem lively or flat? Also think about what activities you have used and how you measured success. Were you able to measure improvement?

2. The work of interactional sociolinguist John Gumperz (1922–2013) did much to help us understand how speakers in cross-cultural situations can misunderstand each other's intent due to different norms in intonation, stress, and non-verbal communication. In your own experience as a teacher and/or language learner, can you recall any experiences in which you have felt uncomfortable in an interaction and perceived that prosodic features may have been to blame?

Chapter 2

A Discourse-Pragmatic Approach to Intonation: An Overview of Brazil's Model of Discourse Intonation

The discourse-pragmatic approach to intonation reconceptualizes traditional pedagogical descriptions of intonation and provides evidence to show that there is a fundamental flaw with presentations that equate intonation primarily with grammatical function or attitudinal expression. While intonation clearly correlates with these components in the discourse, the meaning of the intonation system is not located in the grammatical structure or emotive content of language; thus, it is not wholly predictable based on what is happening in these areas of the language system. Rather, by focusing on these areas, we are essentially picking out pieces of the intonation system and trying to make sense of them individually, rather than looking at the system as a whole.

At the heart of the approach presented here is that the intonation system is essentially **pragmatic** in nature; that is, it contributes independently to the discourse by using intonational cues to link the information to a world or context that the hearer can make sense of. As this context continually changes between speakers and hearers in naturally occurring discourse, this approach recognizes that intonation choices function within a context and lose their significance when this context is reduced or eradicated. This chapter provides an initial overview of the discourse model focusing on both the structure and function of intonation in English. Later chapters discuss each of the systems outlined in more detail. The four basic systems of the model that will be introduced here are:

1. dividing speech into units

2. highlighting prominence information within speech units

3. choosing the pitch pattern on the unit's tonic syllable (or focus word)

4. choosing the pitch height on prominent syllables or the tonic syllable.

2.1. Dividing Speech into Units

In discourse intonation, units of speech are called **tone units**. In pedagogical texts they are also commonly called thought groups, tone groups, sense groups, or intonation units. In all cases, they refer to units of organization in speech that we recognize as having essentially an equivalent function to that of sentences or clauses in writing. Speakers' creation of tone units is guided by their perception of semantic or syntactic chunks of language such as:

◆ one idea or piece of information

◆ a question

◆ one clause (subject + predicate)

◆ division of complex clauses (independent + dependent clauses]

◆ items in a list

◆ adjuncts such as *however* or *finally*.

As an exercise in the processes underlying boundary recognition, read the text shown in Figure 2.1 and predict where you think intonation unit boundaries (or thought groups) might appear.

Figure 2.1.   A Sample Spoken Text without Tone Unit Boundaries

last time I was at an airport I was between planes and I had to make an important phone call I looked around and all the phones were busy so I waited in line and waited and waited finally I began to listen to the conversation of the guy who was talking on the phone I was waiting to use.

Adapted from *Listening in & Speaking Out* by Sharon Bode (1980, p. 10).

Figure 2.2. Sample Showing Pause Boundaries

// last time I was at an airport// I was between planes// and I had to make
an important phone call// I looked around// and all the phones were busy//
so I waited in line// and waited and waited// finally// I began to listen to the
conversation of the guy// who was talking on the phone// I was waiting to use//

Figure 2.3. Another Possible Division of the Text into Intonation Units

// Last time I was at an airport I was between planes and I had to make an
important phone call// I looked around and all the phones were busy// so I waited
in line and waited and waited// finally I began to listen to the conversation of the
guy// who was talking on the phone I was waiting to use//

Figure 2.2 shows one possible division of the text into units (// marks pause boundaries between units); Figure 2.3 shows yet another possibility.

In Figure 2.2, complex clauses are divided into separate units (e.g., // last time I was at an airport// I was between planes//), individual clauses are separated (e.g., // I looked around// all the phones were busy//), repeated items are separated (e.g., // so I waited in line// and waited and waited//), and the adjunct *finally* is separated from the main clause (// finally// I began to listen…).

In Figure 2.3, there are far fewer unit boundaries and syntactic units are much larger (e.g., // last time I was at an airport I was between planes and I had to make an important phone call//); however, each unit continues to make semantic sense as it contains several complete units of information. For example, unit boundaries between "// last time I was at an airport I was// between planes and I had//" would not occur as a possible choice of competent English speakers unless they were having some difficulty with online speech production.

Because there are no absolute rules regarding how a piece of spoken discourse may be divided, speakers do not necessarily always agree on exactly where every tone unit boundary will occur (or is likely to occur) in a piece of text. This happens for a number of reasons including speed of delivery, individual perceptions of how information is most likely to be organized, and other related factors. As with all the systems in the discourse intonation model, the decision lies with the speaker. However, there are unquestionably very likely or very unlikely choices (i.e., expected norms) that unite intonation choice with other aspects of the discourse structure such as syntax or semantics. A given speaker's contributions are designed to be understood and over time, this creates the **conventions** or **norms** that we produce and interpret as speaker-hearers in our speech community. This means that speakers are likely to agree on where unit boundaries are unlikely to appear, such as in the middle of natural semantic and syntactic groupings. (For more detail, see Chapter 3.)

2.2. Highlighting Prominent Information within Tone Units

When we discuss the use of stress in English, the first crucial distinction is the difference between **prominence** (utterance or sentence stress) and **lexical stress** (word stress). The example utterance is taken from a university lecture on U.S. American culture[1] and is marked for word stress using CAPS to indicate each possible lexically stressed syllable (for example, the word *women* has two syllables and is marked for lexical stress on the first syllable *WOmen*).

> //WHAT I WANna DO toDAY IS GIVE YOU AN Overview OF WOmen AND WORK //

This is how the words would be spoken in citation form—that is, as they appear in the dictionary. However, when the utterance is placed in a discourse context (as part of a lecture, for example), the speaker marks only a few prominent syllables as shown in caps and boldface:

> ☏(⦙ // What I wanna do to**DAY** // is give you an **O**verview of **WO**men and **WORK**//

SF 2.1

In other words, not all syllables that receive stress at the lexical level will also receive prominence at the level of the utterance. This is because not all words in a tone unit are given equal importance by the speaker. Let's look at a longer section of the lecture, shown in Figure 2.4.

---

[1]Title: History of the American Family Lecture; transcript ID: LEL105SU113, Michigan Corpus of Academic Spoken English.

Figure 2.4. Extract from a University Lecture Taken from MICASE (LEL105SU113)

1	// what i wanna do today//
2	// is give you an overview of women and work//...
3	// what i will be emphasizing//
4	// is how cultural notions of womanhood//
5	// determine women's work experience okay//....

Figure 2.5. Extract from a University Lecture (MICASE LEL105SU113) Marked for Prominent Syllables

1	// what i wanna do **toDAY**//
2	// is give you an **Overview** of **WOmen** and **WORK**//...
3	// what i will be **EMphasizing**//
4	// is how **CULtural** notions of **WOmanhood**//
5	// **deTERmine** women's **WORK** experience okay//....

SF 2.2

Now read aloud the lecture extract as it is shown in Figure 2.5, which has been divided into its naturally occurring tone units. The words that are emphasized in each unit have been highlighted in bold; these contain the prominent syllables in the unit, which have also been capped.

A speaker's choice of prominence derives from information structure; the more important information a given unit contains, the more prominences are likely to be present. In contrast, many function words (e.g., articles, prepositions, conjunctions) and "low-level" content words (e.g., pronouns, contractions such as *gonna*, or repeated items such as *women* in the lecture extract) that can be anticipated by the hearer are less likely to be emphasized with prominence by the speaker.

It can be useful to think of the typical structure of a tone unit in English as comprising three to seven words and containing one or two prominences. The notion of important information depends on the specific context in which the unit appears, but, in general, it means information that is considered important from the perspective of the speaker—that is, information that the speaker believes the hearer will need in order to understand the meaning and intention of the utterance. (See Chapter 3.)

2.3. Choosing the Pitch Pattern on the Unit's Tonic Syllable

Like the term **tone unit**, the **tonic syllable** is also commonly referred to using different names in the pedagogical literature; some typical choices are focus, nuclear stress, primary accent, or tonic. In Brazil's discourse intonation model, it is termed the **tonic syllable**, and it carries the **tone choice** for the unit; that is, the primary rising, falling, or level pitch movement in the unit. It is the same kind of pitch movement that can appear on other prominent syllables, but the pitch movement is more salient and more sustained. It is usually the syllable in the word that the hearer recognizes as the easiest to hear in terms of length, loudness, and pitch, and it is always the last prominent syllable in the tone unit. In all the transcriptions that follow, it is marked with caps and underlined as shown in this example:

☊⸾ // what I want to do ↗to<u>DAY</u> // is give you an Overview of WOmen and ↘<u>WORK</u>//

SF 2.3

As with all the systems comprising this model, the central tenet guiding tone choice is the speaker's assumptions regarding what information the hearer brings to the interaction. It is in this sense that intonation choices are viewed as, first and foremost, pragmatic in nature. In any given context, the worlds of the speaker and hearer will intersect to differing degrees. The extent of the shared background, or **common ground** assumed between speakers, may be unknown (such as when two strangers begin a conversation), or it may be considerable, such as in the case of interaction between family members. Tone choice summarizes this presumed common ground between speakers at any moment in the interaction.

Five tonal contours make up the Brazil discourse intonation model. They are divided into two opposing pairs: falling (fall and rise-fall) and rising (rise and fall-rise) and a fifth, **neutral tone.** Material that the speaker considers is new/newly asserted is marked with a falling tone, and the speaker marks assumed known/previously suggested material with a rising tone. Recall the essential opposition described in Chapter 1 between Indian English speakers use of a falling tone on // ↘GRAvy//, which was perceived by the British English hearers as an assertion, as opposed to the rising tone choice they expected (// ↗GRAvy//), which would be perceived as a polite suggestion.

The final fifth tone is a level-pitched tone that can also be realized with a slight low rise. Unlike the other four tone choices, the speaker can use this tone to present information as neither shared with nor new to the hearer but simply as a language example. Typically, this fifth, **neutral tone** is used for semi-ritualized or routinized language that is generic rather than specific to a particular interaction. For example, a characteristic use of level tones from classroom discourse includes a teacher's reiteration of well-established procedures or instructions (e.g., // stop ➜WRITing// put your pens ➜DOWN//).

Level tones can also be indicative of the kinds of online production issues that typically occur in natural speech. Spontaneous utterances frequently contain increased hesitation phenomena or fillers such as "// ➜ UH…//" as speakers negotiate real-time speech production. This tone may also be used to signal and mitigate disagreement, as in "// ➜ UM // ➜WELL…//," which can be glossed as something like "I'm about to disagree with you, and I want to give you a warning."

Although it is important to remember that a speaker's tone choices are under individual control and dependent on situational context, analysis of natural language occurrences shows that speakers of Traditional Englishes will vary their tone choices in a consistent manner using primarily falling tones with some rising and level tones mixed in (Cauldwell, 2003; Pickering, 2001). This will be explored in greater detail in Chapter 4.

2.4. Choosing the Pitch Level on Prominent Syllables or the Tonic Syllable

The final system comprising discourse intonation is key and termination. As both are concerned with pitch height (rather than movement) and appear on prominent syllables, they are addressed together. Key and termination describe the systematic way in which speakers conventionally use the **pitch range** of their voice. In discourse intonation, Brazil proposes that we use a small number of pitch contrasts to convey linguistic meaning. Each speaker's overall range is divided into three levels: high (H), mid (M), and low (L). **Key** choice is marked on the first prominence in the unit, and **termination** is marked on the **tonic syllable** (the final prominent syllable). In tone units in which there is only one prominent syllable (the tonic syllable), both key and termination choice fall on that syllable. This would be the case in tone units that comprised only one word, for example.

Pitch range plays an important role in cueing the opening and closing of interactions. Consider the type of interaction that commonly appears in classroom discourse. This example shows a typical three-part teacher-student inter-action, often called an Initiation-Response-Feedback (IRF) pattern, in which the teacher both opens and closes the interaction by posing a question and evaluating the student's response:

> T(eacher):   What's the final answer?
>
> S(tudent):   Twelve
>
> T(eacher):   Twelve, good.

This short interaction can be marked for probable tone units and probable tone choices on the tonic syllable of each unit, as shown:

(((T: // WHAT'S the final ↗ANSwer//

      S: // ↘TWELVE// (or ↗TWELVE//)

      T: // TWELVE ↘GOOD//

SF 2.4

Note that the student response could be either // ↘TWELVE// with a falling tone or // ↗ TWELVE// with a rising tone (the sound file plays both options in full in succession). In the first case, the student is <u>stating</u> the answer as a confident assertion, whereas in the second, the student is instead <u>checking</u> that the teacher agrees with the response as she may be less confident of the answer.

In addition to predicting probable tone choices on the tonic syllable (e.g., ANSwer, TWELVE, and GOOD), we can also predict choice of pitch height on all the prominent syllables in the interaction (e.g., key choice on WHAT and TWELVE and termination choice on ANSwer, TWELVE, and GOOD.) Note that this is shown by using a different kind of arrow with ⇑ for high pitch, ⇨ for mid pitch, and ⇓ for low pitch:

(((T: // ⇨WHAT'S the final ⇨ANSwer//

      S: // ⇨ TWELVE //

      T: // ⇨TWELVE ⇓GOOD//

SF 2.5

The transcription of key and termination given matches the conventional choices we would anticipate in a typical IRF exchange between a teacher and student. The first key and termination choices on WHAT and <u>ANS</u>wer are given in a mid, or neutral, key or pitch. If the teacher had asked the question with a high termination instead (e.g., T: // what's the final ⇧<u>ANS</u>wer//), the use of this unusually high pitch would sound unexpected and inappropriately aggressive in this context. The student responds with a similar mid-level neutral termination choice "// ⇨ <u>TWELVE</u>//," which agrees with the teacher's mid-level choice and glosses as "I think it's twelve; I think you'll agree with me?"

It is often easier to understand the significance of these pitch level choices if we speculate on the communicative value of either of the other two choices if used by the student—that is, high or low termination. A high termination of "// ⇧<u>TWELVE</u>//" in response to the teacher's mid key would sound unnecessarily combative. It might be glossed as "I think it's twelve; are you going to contradict me?" If the student had chosen a low termination instead (e.g., // ⇩ <u>TWELVE</u>//), this would indicate a closing of the interaction and gloss as "I know the answer is twelve; I'm ending this interaction." This would also be problematic as typically we would expect the teacher, not the student, to indicate when the interaction is over.

In the final turn in the interaction, the teacher uses both a mid key choice of "⇨TWELVE" and a low termination choice of "⇩<u>GOOD</u>." The first prominent syllable (⇨TWELVE) is the **onset** syllable and its neutral, mid key can be glossed as "I agree with you; the answer is twelve." The low termination value on the final underlined **tonic syllable** (⇩<u>GOOD</u>) indicates that the exchange is complete. As noted, in this context, the third move in the exchange (other than a sign of assent from the student) is the teacher's prerogative. The teacher may choose, for example, to end the interaction with a simple mid termination indicating agreement or end the exchange as shown with a low termination closure on "//⇩ <u>GOOD</u>//."

2.5. A Competing Model: The Autosegmental-Metrical Approach

Although this book introduces Brazil's model, it's important to briefly address a competing model in current intonation study that is used particularly in the United States. The **Autosegmental-Metrical approach** (Pierrehumbert & Hirschberg, 1990) has its beginnings in the U.S. and although it can be argued that the model has yet to make a significant impact on pedagogical practice, it has made a considerable impact on intonation research and is now widely cited at least, in part, because it is the basis for a popular system of intonational transcription called **ToBI,** or Tone and Break Indices.

The Autosegmental-Metrical (AM) model is discussed here for two reasons. First, students and practitioners who are new to this part of the field and are exposed to both models can become quickly confused by the different terminology that each model uses. In fact, there is much that can be considered as functionally equivalent for a pedagogical (rather than a theoretical) context. Second, there are important areas of agreement between the models regarding the meaning or function of intonation in discourse that unite the models and the field of intonology as it is currently understood.[2]

With regard to the function of the intonation system, both Brazil and Pierrehumbert & Hirschberg agree on two fundamentally important concepts. The first is that the system operates concurrently with the other language systems present in spoken discourse yet is independent of them. In other words, intonation choices make a unique contribution to the communicative value of the utterance; therefore, they are neither predetermined nor rendered redundant by either grammatical structure or lexical choice. A second area of agreement is that the systematic use of intonation extends beyond individual components such as a single pitch movement and has independent implications for the structure of the discourse overall. The speaker is involved in a continuous assessment of the relationship between the message and the hearer. As this is constantly changing, intonation choices are relevant only at the moment of speaking and to the particular participants involved in the discourse. In other words, the focus is not on the intonation choices in isolation but on how these are perceived by the hearer in relation to other parts of the discourse.

Let's consider an example: Brazil proposes that a low termination tonic syllable signals the close of an interaction to cue the end of the teacher-student IRF exchange. Pierrehumbert & Hirschberg describe the same phenomenon as "not forward looking" (p. 305)—that is, as potentially closing off a section of the discourse. Thus, both begin to build up a picture of intonational choices that are determined by the speaker and defined in relation to each other.

Important differences lie in the structures that comprise the model and this is also where terminology varies. Unlike the five tones described in Brazil's framework, the AM model comprises a series of static tones or tonal targets that determine the final shape of the pitch contour. There are two groups of tones: pitch accents (marked with *) and phrasal or final boundary tones (marked

---

[2]The following discussion is based on Pierrehumbert & Hirschberg's (1990) paper "The Meaning of Intonational Contours in the Interpretation of Discourse," in which the authors focus specifically on intonational meaning in discourse.

with %). Functionally, however, many of the tonal combinations that are cre-ated by these alternative systems have meanings attached to them that are simi-lar to Brazil's interpretations of identical overall pitch movements. For example, this contour—an H^* pitch accent followed by an L phrase accent and an L% boundary tone—is said to "convey new information" in AM:

Legumes are a good source of vitamins
                    H*   L L%

(Pierrehumbert & Hirschberg, 1990, p. 272)

The shape of the H*LL% contour is equivalent to Brazil's falling tone, which also adds a new information to the interaction:

// leGUMES are a good source of ↘Vltamins//

At this level of comparison, there is clearly a strong resemblance between the two models in their mutual conception of the function of intonation in dis-course, and how these are realized in terms of associated pitch values. However, there are also important differences that become evident when the models are applied pedagogically. Although these are not discussed here in the interests of space, the interested reader can find them described in Pickering (1999) and Wennerstrom (2001).

2.6. Which Model Should You Choose?

There are both theoretical and practical reasons why a teacher or researcher interested in intonation might chose one model over another (such as AM rather than Brazil or vice versa). It is certainly the case that no model can claim to represent some kind of absolute truth, and thus each must be considered on other merits. For teachers, it may be as simple as choosing the one that they learned as a student and that they are most comfortable and familiar with. Researchers may consider how well the system describes their data. For exam-ple, when the theoretical categories described are applied to actual speech data, how much of the data do not fit or go unexplained? A model that leaves a great deal of data unexplained is not descriptively adequate and is not likely to be the best at hand. A teacher will similarly be looking for a model that has strong predictive power with regard to the patterns that are found in everyday, natu-rally occurring speech with which their students must become familiar. In addition, teachers are looking for something that they view as teachable and learnable for their students (see Chapter 9). As both a teacher and researcher, I have chosen to work with Brazil's model for several reasons:

1. Of the currently available models of discourse intonation, all of which outstrip traditional pedagogical presentations, I find it the most usable system of transcription and the most insightful metalanguage in describing the choices speakers make. As Cauldwell (2002) notes, it is a comprehensive approach to both the analysis and teaching of real, everyday speech that comprises "a theory, a set of categories and realizations, a notation and transcription practice." (p. 24)

2. It has been applied effectively to a number of different varieties of English including second language learner English, thus it has proven value in the ESL/EFL contexts. Some examples include the investigation of English language learners from Germany (Koester, 1990), Italy (Pirt, 1990), and Korea, Greece, and Indonesia (Hewings, 1995). In addition, a number of pronunciation texts have been based on its tenets (Bradford, 1988; Cauldwell, 2012, 2013; Gorsuch et al., 2013).

3. Brazil developed the model with classroom discourse in mind (see for example, Brazil, Coulthard, & Johns, 1980), and it has been consistently applied in this and other crucial cross-cultural and professional contexts (Cheng, Greaves & Warren, 2008; Pickering 2001, 2004; Staples, 2014).

2.7. Summary

This chapter has provided an overview of the discourse intonation model that will be examined in detail throughout the book. Before moving on, however, it is important to reiterate two crucial issues that we will continue to come back to throughout the text. First, it is easier to understand that the intonation system is systematic if you view it through **discourse** as opposed to through isolated or partial utterances. Choices in the prominence, tone, and key and termination areas interact with each other, the specific context of the interaction, and the perceived relationship between speaker and hearer. When we isolate these choices from one another, it becomes much harder to see intonation as a system in the same way as we might see the syntactic system. A speaker's choice of a rising tone, for example, is analogous to the choice of a noun as opposed to a verb: Each is defined in relation to other parts of the model.

Second, it is easier to work with intonation if you view it as a probabilistic system rather than as a deterministic system. In other words, given enough knowledge of the context of the interaction and the speakers involved, we can predict what is likely (or conversely, unlikely) to happen, but we cannot predict it in absolute terms. Ultimately, individual speakers decide what they want to say and how they want to say it. They are not constrained by what we might expect to hear. Speakers may also want to exploit inherent ambiguities in the system or even deliberately mislead their hearer. Alternatively, they may realize only after they have uttered a tone unit that a choice they have made has been perceived wrongly by the hearer. I am sure every reader can recall at least one time where they or someone they know remarked, "Oh, no, I didn't mean it like that!"

2.8. Check Your Learning

1. How many systems comprise Brazil's model of discourse intonation as a whole?

2. Consider the separate systems outlined in the chapter and answer these questions:

   ◇ What is a tone unit and how is it identified?

   ◇ What is the difference between word stress and prominence?

   ◇ What is the tonic syllable in Brazil's model?

   ◇ What are the five tonal contours in Brazil's model?

   ◇ Key and termination are both concerned with what prosodic feature?

   ◇ What is the difference between *key* and *termination*?

3. Explain one difference and one similarity between Brazil's framework and Pierrehumbert & Hirschberg's model.

2.9. Activities

1. At the beginning of this chapter, we used an example from the Michigan Corpus of Academic Spoken English (MICASE) (Simpson, Briggs, Ovens, & Swales, 2002). This corpus was created at the English Language Institute at the University of Michigan from 1997–2001. It comprises more than a million words of transcribed academic speech events of all kinds. Written transcripts are freely available on the internet (https://quod.lib.umich.edu/m/micase), and some sound files are also available (https://media.talkbank.org/CABank/MICASE). As we will continue to use these data, take the opportunity now to browse these sites and learn how to navigate them.

2. As we noted in this chapter, word (lexical) stress and utterance stress (prominence) are two different prosodic features. It is the case, however, that if a word receives prominence, the prominence will appear on the syllable that normally receives the lexical stress in its citation form (for example, if the word *women* was made prominent, the prominent syllable would be the first, lexically stressed syllable *WOmen*.)

   Word stress is difficult to predict in Traditional Englishes, largely due to differences in word origins. Germanic words, for example, typically have their primary stress on the first syllable; whereas words with a French origin may keep their original stress pattern: gaRAGE and balLET in General American English. However, they may also be changed over time; for example, both words are pronounced with stress on the first syllable in British English: GARage and BALlet. Despite a broad set of patterns, native speakers prefer certain patterns to others, and the longer the word remains as part of English, the greater the tendency for the stress to shift to the beginning of the word (Celce-Murcia et al., 1996, p. 136, ftn. 7).

   One interesting way to test this is to write a word that native speakers of Traditional Englishes may not know (try Kissimmee—the name of a city in Florida) and ask speakers how they would say that word. Nine out of ten speakers will say KISSimee with a stress on the first syllable. The city is actually pronounced KisSIMmee with a stress on the middle syllable and probably derived from a local Native American word. These preferences for particular patterns are very tacit, and native speakers often do not realize that they are rule- or norm-governed. As an example, identify the stress on these pairs and triplets of words and formulate the rule regarding primary stress.[3]

The farm was used to produce produce.

The dump was so full that it had to refuse more refuse.

The soldier decided to desert his dessert in the desert.

Since there is no time like the present, he thought it was time to present the present.

I did not object to the object.

The insurance was invalid for the invalid.

I had to subject the subject to a series of tests.

How can I intimate this to my most intimate friend?

And here's another example of the same stress pattern from *Amsterdam* by Ian McEwan:

In a language as idiomatically stressed as English, opportunities

for misreadings are bound to arise. By a mere backward

movement of stress, a verb can become a noun, an act a thing.

To refuse, to insist on saying no to what you believe is wrong,

becomes at a stroke refuse, an insurmountable pile of garbage.

(2010, p. 70).

---

[3]With thanks to Jackie Payton for sharing this example.

Chapter 3

Segmenting the Speech Stream: Tone Units

This chapter focuses on the division of the speech stream into semantically meaningful groupings of words, or **tone units**. They are also sometimes referred to as thought groups, sense groups, breath groups, tone groups, or intonational phrases or groups. Tone units are marked prosodically using some combination of prominence and pausing. We will look at some of the different ways in which these groups are typically characterized and how we define them. We go on to look at the closely related area of rhythm in spoken discourse. Finally, we look at these issues in light of what English language students may find difficult and consider some implications for instruction.

As discussed, the tone unit structure that comprises spoken text can be described as having a similar function to sentence structure in written text. Without tone units, it is very difficult for the hearer to organize the stream of speech into separate, meaningful parts. The comparison between written and spoken units can be somewhat misleading, however, because, unlike written discourse, the rules as to what constitutes a single unit in spoken discourse are very flexible. In these examples, a complete unit is shown in each case between the slashes (//):

- // uh //

- // dude//

- // let's take a look at the book//

- // I have two daughters aged five and eight//and when I see the plans for this memorial// I think about what it will be like when I first bring them here//upon the memorial's completion// (Obama, 2006)

In spontaneous, everyday speech, a single hesitation marker such as *uh* or an exclamation *dude!* may comprise an entire unit if it is marked as a prominent tonic syllable. In contrast, in a prepared speech, a tone unit may comprise a complete syntactic or semantic chunk of seven or eight words and a much longer melodic contour. This chapter looks at the machinery by which competent speaker-hearers of English recognize this unit structure in spoken discourse. The two crucial elements are prominence and pausing.

3.1. Prominence

The feature of prominence (indicated in transcription by using CAPS) is marked by increased pitch, length, and volume on the primary stressed syllable in the prominent word, and it signals a meaningful choice by the speaker to emphasize particular information in the tone unit. A complete tone unit comprises at a minimum, one prominent syllable called the **tonic syllable** (indicated by using CAPS and underlined). Typically, however, it will also contain a prominent **onset** syllable. Let's look at an example of the way in which information is signaled using onset and tonic syllable prominence based on the pragmatic intentions of the speaker. If we take a tone unit such as *a package of books sits on the table*, at least two possible prominence selections could be made:

A.   // a package of BOOKS sits on the TAble//

B.   // a PACKage of books sits on the TAble//

SF 3.1

In (A) the speaker places the initial onset prominence on *BOOKS*. This highlights books as the important information as opposed to perhaps flowers or cups. The tonic prominence highlights the location—that is, on the table, as opposed to on the floor or on the chair. The choice of prominence on syllables of both words projects a context in which both these pieces of information are new or unrecoverable from the prior discourse context.

Equally, by choosing not to make prominent certain other words in the unit, the speaker assumes that the information is recoverable for the hearer from either the linguistic or non-linguistic context. For example, within a non-linguistic context, a choice of *box* instead of *package* is also possible but in this context, these terms are seen as synonymous. In addition, books can be assumed to *sit* on the table as opposed to *stand up*. Within a linguistic context, constraints in the language system apply to the functions words *a* and *of* which means they also do not need to be made prominent.

In (B) the speaker chooses to make *PACKAGE* prominent and *books* non-prominent. This choice of prominence projects a context in which both package and table are new or unrecoverable from the prior discourse, but that books is old or given information, i.e. recoverable or already understood from the context of the interaction. For example:

   A.   // was there a <u>BOOK</u> there//

     B.   // there was a <u>PACK</u>age of books there//

SF 3.2

These prominences frame the **tonic segment** of the tone unit, which is the obligatory meaning-bearing element of the unit. A minimal tonic segment (the smallest possible complete tone unit) comprises only a tonic syllable and the surrounding unstressed material, such as in "// was there a <u>BOOK</u> there//." An extended tonic segment can include multiple **intermediate prominences** in addition to the onset and tonic prominences. An example is "// WHY can you NEver MAKE up your <u>MIND</u>//," in which NEver and MAKE are intermediate prominences.

Prominence has a number of frequent informational functions that are typically highlighted in teaching texts. These examples are adapted from Sue Miller's *Targeting Pronunciation* (2000):

   1. Highlighting new information, as in:

   A: I need to borrow some MOney. (*money* is the new information)

     B: How MUCH money? (prominence shifts to *much* because money is now old information)

SF 3.3

Note that a good way to practice hearing the difference is to try saying the unit with the prominence shifted to non-crucial or repeated information (as in B) and notice how confusing it becomes, for example:

   A: I need to borrow some MOney.

     B: How much MOney?

SF 3.4

2. Establishing a contrast, as in:

🦻⑴ A: Don't we have a staff meeting today?

B: No, it's not a STAFF meeting. It's a diRECtor's meeting.

SF 3.5

3. Contradicting a previous contribution, as in:

🦻⑴ A: There were two other people WAITing.

B: Are you sure? I thought there were THREE people waiting.

SF 3.6

4. Showing enthusiastic agreement, as in:

🦻⑴ A: That was a GREAT movie!

B: That WAS a great movie!

SF 3.7

As with all the systems in the Brazil model, choices of prominence lie with the speaker, who will align their choices with the conventions or norms in the language unless there is a specific reason not to. However, depending on the variety of English that the speaker is familiar with, these conventions or norms may be quite different. An example is given in Figure 3.1.

Read Dialogue 1 aloud with prominence on the capped syllables. If you are a speaker of a Traditional English variety (e.g., British or American English), you will probably find it difficult to read aloud the prominence marked in B because your natural reaction will be to highlight the important contrast (*golf* vs. *small*), as shown in Dialogue 2.

Figure 3.1. Prominence Choices

🦻⑴
| Dialogue 1: |
| A: Did you want to take the small umBRELla? |
| B: No, the golf umBRELla. |
| |
| Dialogue 2: |
| A: Did you want to take the small umBRELla? |
| B: No, the GOLF umbrella. |

SF 3.8

Conversely, other varieties of English (New or Emerging varieties) and other languages may indicate this kind of contrast entirely differently, such as by not using prominence patterns to indicate this information structure but by using some other linguistic device such as syntactic movement or some kind of marker (see Chapters 7 and 8). It is partially these familiar patterns that give different varieties of English the rhythm that we recognize and expect them to have (see Section 3.3).

3.2. Pausing

Pausing is perhaps the most intuitive boundary marker. In fact, the salience of pausing as a cue to a tone unit depends in large part on the speech genre in question. In the case of public speaking, pausing often is the most important cue to separating tone units; however, this is frequently not the case in faster-paced conversational speech where more than one tonic segment (as indicated by pitch prominence) can appear without an intervening pause. Thus, pausing is not a necessary cue to tone units even though it is a very typical one.

Let's look at two examples of different speech genres to show how this cue can vary. The first example is taken from a speech made by Princess Diana in 1993 in support of resources for women with mental health needs:

> Where// do we begin// from those// I have spoken to through my work with 'Turning Point'// the beginning seems to be// that women in our society are seen as the carers// whatever life throws at them// they will always cope// on call// twenty four hours a day// seven days a week// whether their children are sick// their husbands are out of work// or their parents are old and frail// and need attending//

In this prepared speech, Princess Diana speaks with long pauses between each of the units. Typically units are approximately five words long although in some cases there are rhetorical or dramatic pauses that divide the discourse into even smaller units such as in her opening: // Where// do we begin//.

In contrast, at the extreme opposite end of speech samples we might hear, we find a talking style described as "motormouth interrupt."[1] This conversational

---

[1] Information taken from Motormouth Interrupt: http://changingminds.org/techniques/conversation/interrupting/interruption_techniques.htm

technique is a way of interrupting someone by talking quickly; some suggest that the speaker should "find a small pause…and then jump in and do not stop":

> Find a small pause, for example when they are taking a breath, and then jump in and do not stop. Do not give them time to interrupt back. Just keep on talking without pause. Also be careful not to send any signals that will allow them to pick up on a way back in. Sometimes it is even a good idea not to look directly at them.

As an example, there is a transcription of the following speech sample:

> //Omygoddidyouseethat!Idon'tknowifyouaregoingtogoouttonightbutIreally wanto… //

Because discourse intonation relies on pitch cues in tone unit division, Brazil does not elaborate on pause patterns apart from noting that they may and frequently do coincide with tone units. But it is important to remember that pause length and frequency varies with discourse genre. Because of these genre specific differences, it is difficult to pinpoint the importance of precise pause lengths or the exact amount and placement of filled and unfilled pauses. As with many other aspects of prosody, it is easier to identify what sounds disfluent and look at the characteristics of those speech patterns. It is clear that competent speakers of English have a sense of what does not sound fluent in their variety.

3.3. Rhythm in Spoken Discourse

Rhythm is closely related to tone unit structure and prominence patterns. For example, typical reductions in connected speech in Traditional varieties of English such as linking, assimilation, or deletion contribute to the typical shape of tone units and the perceptions of the hearer(s). Language varieties have a unique rhythm that has been shown to be distinguishable by hearers in the experimental literature (Ohala & Gilbert, 1981; Ramus & Mehler, 1999). Precisely what these differences are and exactly how they should be described is still debated (see, for example, Dauer, 1983; Marks, 1999). Traditionally, however, within an ESL/EFL context the rhythmic properties of different languages have been described from a very early stage as either **stress-timed** or **syllable-timed** languages. Originally proposed by Abercrombie (1967), stress-timed rhythm defined languages in which regular beats occur on stressed syllables and unstressed syllables are "squeezed" between them. In contrast, in a language with a syllable-timed rhythm, the beats occur on each syllable and thus syllables tend to be more equal in length. Although this distinction can still be seen in the pedagogical literature (see, for example, Celce-Murcia et al., 2010, p. 208), it has come increasingly under criticism for its perceived over-simplification of rhythmic differences, and in fact, the distinction may obscure the reality of the rhythmic patterns found in spontaneous speech. Cauldwell (2002) argues that spontaneous speech is not as regularized as stress-timed models suggest and proposes that the constraints of real-time speech ultimately control the rhythm of speech:

> The suprasegmental choices that speakers make (speed of delivery, size of tone-unit, pitch-height, tone-choice, volume), and performance factors inevitable in unscripted speech (pauses, restarts, etc.) are the dominant factors in determining the rhythm. (p. 7)

Cauldwell further notes that the "rare patches" of highly regularized rhythm (such as what you find in a nursery rhyme) that we might present to our students are more likely to be the result of a deliberate rhythmic choice on the part of the speaker to indicate **formulaic** or **prepackaged chunks** of language (e.g., proverbs such as // you can LEAD a HORSE to WAter but you CAN'T make it DRINK//). They may also be coincidental; that is, the speaker just happens to produce a longer tone unit with periodic stresses.

In fact, as prominences increase in an individual tone unit, a more isochronous rhythm is created that sounds more sing-song or emphatic. Bolinger (1986) calls this **stylized intonation** and describes it as something that is problematic if it is the exclusive focus in the ESL/EFL context:

> I have a suspicion that this sort of singsong is just the kind of intonational frame that a classroom drill is apt to fall into. If so, it has helped to make us see English accentual rhythm as more regular than it really is. (p. 48)

This is indeed what happens in many ESL/EFL classrooms. Presentations designed to work on rhythm or stress patterns are often taught through the use of nursery rhymes and poems that do not reflect the reality of the rhythmic patterns found in naturally occurring spoken discourse. Clennell (1997) suggests that this pattern can be so pervasive in language learner speech that speakers "effectively 'neuter' the pragmatic intention of the utterance" (p. 119).

Nevertheless, it is clear that as speakers and listeners, we do perceive that languages have different rhythmic structures and that we can to some extent discriminate between them (Nazzi & Ramus, 2003). Working within a discourse intonation framework, a more productive way to view these differences is to recognize that the conventions that underlie the way in which information is organized in any given language often result in typical prominence selections that sound familiar to speaker-hearers of that variety. In Traditional varieties of English, the suspension bridge contour described by Bolinger (1961, p. 136) and shown in Figure 3.2 demonstrates one of the most commonly occurring prominence patterns found across tone units.

The "bridge" represents an onset prominence at the beginning of the unit and a tonic syllable prominence at the end of the unit, with non-prominent syllables in the middle. Some simple examples are:

👂 // I REAlly liked the MOvie//

    // it's the FIRST thing we did in the CLASS//

    // do you KNOW what STREET it's on//

SF 3.9

In spoken texts, Cauldwell (2002) found that almost 90 percent of tone units contained one or two prominences while triple-prominence units accounted for only 5 percent and only one quadruple prominence appeared in a total of 1,603 tone units.

Of course, more complex information sequencing within and across units also has an effect on what prominence selections are more likely to appear and thus sound familiar. An example of this kind of patterning in Traditional English varieties is shown in the expression of explicit contrasts. In these units, the contrast between *acidity* and *alkalinity* is emphasized using prominence struc-

Figure 3.2. The Suspension Bridge Contour

ture to contrast *lower* with *larger* and *acid* with *base*. Before you listen to the audio, read this extract aloud and focus on the prominences. You will hear the repeated prominence patterns across the tone units.

◠⑾ // We use the pH meter to MEAsure the aCIdity or alkaLINity of
    COMpounds// if the pH value is LOwer than SEven// then it's an
    Acid/ if the value is LARger than SEven// then it's a BASE//.

(Levis & Pickering, 2004, p. 507)

SF 3.10

3.4. Summary and Pedagogical Implications

This chapter has introduced the first two of the four basic systems in the discourse intonation model: (1) the division of speech into units and (2) the choice of prominent syllables within those units. It has focused on the two prosodic characteristics that comprise these systems: prominence and pausing. Although the division of speech into units and the notion of speech rhythm may be familiar concepts to readers, it is important to remember that they are conceptualized in a very particular way within the discourse intonation model. Terms such as prominence and tone unit have particular definitions that may be less familiar and that will be reiterated in subsequent chapters.

There are a number of common problems that second language learners often experience as they work to create fluent unit structure with appropriate prominences in English. These are particularly evident in the beginning to intermediate stages of development in which learner discourse typically exhibits these characteristics:

- Short tone units with multiple prominences that make it difficult for the listener to focus on the onset and tonic syllables

- Erratic pause patterns with highly variable pause placement and pause lengths that then disrupt melodic contours

- Overly regularized, unnatural rhythmic patterns that can obscure information structure.

Clearly, fluency is at least in part a matter of practice and confidence. The more confident learners feel in regard to their language ability, the more fluent we hope they will become. However, that does not mean that we can assume that their understanding of the nature of prominence structure in English or rhythmicality will simply emerge along the way by osmosis; and for many learners, it does not.

In light of the discourse intonation model introduced here, we might want to reconsider how we approach intonation instruction overall. For example, traditional descriptions of syllable stress usually focus on word-level production. Learners are also commonly advised to stress content words but not function words. Emphasizing the production of individual words and utterances outside of meaningful discourse interaction may, in fact, exacerbate the problem of learner production of too many prominences within a tone unit and contribute to a form of **teacher-induced error** (Richmond, 1984; Stenson, 1983), in which learners are encouraged to create the patterns that will obscure the meaning of their utterances. Thus it is important for students to practice stress in longer meaningful chunks within a specific discourse context.

3.5. Check Your Learning

1. What are the two most important prosodic features to consider when examining tone unit structure?

2. Why is it important to consider discourse genre when looking at pause structure in speech?

3. Why is it important to focus on naturally occurring discourse when thinking about speech rhythm?

3.6. Activities

1. This text[2] is an old grammarian joke based on pause structure that is fun to read aloud. Read each version aloud with pauses between the tone units and discuss the different meanings.

What Love Is All About

Version 1:

Dear John//I want a man who knows what love is all about. //You are generous, kind, thoughtful. //People who are not like you admit to being useless and inferior. //You have ruined me for other men. //I yearn for you. //I have no feelings whatsoever when we're apart. //I can be forever happy—will you let me be yours? //Jane//

Version 2:

Dear John//I want a man who knows what love is. //All about you are generous, kind, thoughtful people, who are not like you. //Admit to being useless and inferior. //You have ruined me. //For other men, I yearn. //For you, I have no feelings whatsoever. //When we're apart, I can be forever happy. //Will you let me be? //Yours, //Jane//

2. Discuss how the length and distribution of a speaker's pauses might vary in these contexts:

    ◊   in general conversational interaction as opposed to formal speeches

---

[2]Taken from Nordquist: www.infoplease.com/language-arts/grammar-and-spelling/punctuation-punctuation-matters

◇ reading a story aloud in contrast to telling a story spontaneously

◇ in the speech of someone who is emotionally very agitated in contrast to someone who is very calm.

3. We noted that the pragmatic function of prominence is to project the speaker's understanding of whether something should be already understood (non-prominent) or is new information (prominent). One way that this can be demonstrated is by examining **mishearings**, or **prosodic repairs** (Cutler, 1983). Describe how this is exemplified in this example in which the second speaker has misunderstood the first, and what conversational repair will be required:

   A: //which <u>ACE</u> did you play//

   B: //the eight of <u>HEARTS</u>//

   (Brazil, 1997, p. 27)

4. Unlike the production of prominences in spontaneous speech, which is context-dependent, prominence structure can also be routinized. The English language is full of conventionalized prominence patterns that have become stylized on routinized lexical phrases. Describe the prominence patterns of these conventionalized phrases noted by Ashby and Ashby (1995):

   ◇ the way we repeat phone numbers

   ◇ the way words are spelled aloud

   ◇ the way we commonly list items.

Then practice with your own name and phone number.

Chapter 4

Identifying New and Old Information: Tone Choice

This chapter addresses the third system in Brazil's model, the tonal system or the pitch movement on the final tonic syllable in each unit. This chapter discusses the overall pragmatic functions of falling tones (fall, rise-fall) and rising tones (rise, fall-rise) and the final, level tone. So as not to overwhelm, Chapter 6 will discuss the differences between types of falling tones and rising tones (e.g., the pragmatic function of the use of a falling tone versus a rise-fall tone).

4.1. Pitch and Pragmatic Meaning

Tone choice is the system that ESL/EFL practitioners are most likely to be familiar with because this pitch movement is commonly referred to as the tonal contour (in the British tradition) or as the final or terminal contour (in the American tradition). Historically, in ESL/EFL materials, tone choice is typically described as having a primarily grammatical function—for example, that a statement ends with a falling pitch and a yes-no question ends with a rising pitch. However, it is now recognized that this kind of grammatically based description does not hold up well when examining intonation in a naturally occurring discourse context:

> Currently, intonation teaching tends to be limited to rising and falling patterns at the ends of sentences, with a direct connection to grammatical form. This limited account does not reflect normal spoken discourse, in which intonation continues a spoken turn or ends it, signals idea boundaries, achieves cohesion, and builds rapport. (Levis, 2016, p. 428)

Within a discourse-pragmatic model, the grammatical meanings traditionally associated with the use of certain tones are subsumed under a larger umbrella that incorporates but is not limited to grammatical function. In other words, we can posit overall pragmatic functions for rising and falling tone choices that allow us to explain their grammatical functions without relying on syntactic structure (we will look more closely at question types in Section 4.2). Table 4.1 summarizes the discourse-pragmatic assumptions associated with the five tonal contours that comprise Brazil's model.

Putting aside the level tone for the moment, in general terms, tone choice summarizes the common ground between speakers—that is, what is assumed by the listeners to be known and unknown in the context of any given interaction. It is only within this context that the communicative value of any particular tone choice can be derived. The four rising and falling patterns are divided into two opposing pairs. Tones that end in a falling movement are designated

Table 4.1 Pragmatic Assumptions Associated with Particular Tone Choices by Speakers and Hearers

Falling Tones ↘ and ↗↘ (Fall and Rise-Fall)	Rising Tones ↗ and ↘↗ (Rise and Fall-Rise)	Level Tone → (Flat or a Slight Rise)
This is a new assertion or statement, and is world-changing—e.g., *I'm telling you something new*	This is part of our shared background, and is part of your world view—e.g., *I'm reminding you of something you know*	I'm (temporarily) withdrawing from this negotiation, and am making no assumptions—e.g., *I'm not indicating whether I think you know this or not*
I've finished my act of "telling"—e.g., *I've completed my message*	I'm continuing or linking this to what I said before—e.g., *this is part of the same message*	This is a language sample—e.g., *I'm not focused on the communicative message*
I'm highlighting my role as authority—e.g., *I am demonstrating my superior knowledge*	I'm building solidarity—e.g., *I am highlighting my hearer's possible knowledge*	I am not focused on my hearer—e.g., *I am not concerned with my hearer's knowledge*
Exclusivity—e.g., *the speaker is focused on themselves*	Inclusivity—e.g., *the speaker is focused on the hearer*	Neutral—e.g., *The speaker is focused only on the language*

as **proclaiming tones** (p = ↘; p+ =↗↘). Proclaiming tones have an overall semantic sense of declaring the material or information in the unit as new (e.g., "I am telling you something I assume is world-changing"), asserted, or incontrovertible (e.g., "I'm telling you this fact"). Thus, we can think of their meaning as correlating with verbs such as *assert, tell, complete, command, instruct,* and so on.

In contrast, tones that end in a rising movement are designated as **referring tones** (r = ↘↗; r+ = ↗) and declare the material or information in the unit as in some way already conversationally in play (e.g. "I'm reminding you that you know this, or that I think you should know this"). The reminder can come from the ongoing discourse or the general linguistic or situational context. The meaning of referring tones can be usefully correlated with verbs such as *remind, reflect, include, confirm,* or *continue.*

Through their tone choices (i.e., what information is proclaimed as opposed to referred to), speakers negotiate toward a state of convergence (or coming together) with their hearers. In this way, a roughly mutual understanding of the discourse message is achieved between speaker and listeners. This notion of convergence includes not just information but also convergence of a social nature—that is, speakers can decrease the affective distance between themselves and their hearers by projecting a broader common ground that is more inclusive of the hearer and thus more cooperative and more likely to lead to successful interaction. An example of this kind of projection is often used by restaurant managers when they come over to diners to check that all is well. Typically they will say:

🎧 // does everything ↗TASTE ok//
SF 4.1

The use of the rising tone in this context means "I'd like to confirm that everything tastes ok" rather than the choice of a falling tone, which would mean "I'm asking, does it taste ok or doesn't it taste ok?" In the prior case, a rising tone can be a clever way to "prompt" the diner to respond positively as the speaker would otherwise have to overtly disagree with the underlying assumption, as in "Well, actually no, it doesn't...." These utterances also often have a **phatic** (relationship-building) purpose, and are a form of social bridge-building in which the primary intent is more to do with confirmation of comfort than a genuine request for information (Brazil, 1997) (see Section 4.3).

4.2. Question Types and Falling and Rising Tones

Because of their frequency in ESL/EFL materials let's consider the pragmatic opposition of falling and rising tone choices in the specific context of questions. As a reminder, a typical ESL/EFL pedagogical presentation of grammatical function will include the intonational rule that yes/no questions (A) appear with a final rising tone while *wh-* questions (B) will appear with a final falling tone:

A: // ARE you ↗LEAVing//

B: // WHY are you ↘LEAVing//

SF 4.2

If we begin instead from the discourse-pragmatic definitions of rising and falling tones, we can assume these were the communicative intents of each:

A: // Are you ↗LEAVing// means "It looks like you are leaving. Can you confirm that I am correct?"

B: // WHY are you ↘LEAVing// means "I can see that you are leaving, but I don't know why so please tell me."

In A, the speaker is probably making an assumption based on some action being undertaken by the hearer (maybe the person is packing their bag or gathering their coat). In this case, the actions of the hearer (which the speaker can see) function to create common ground or a presumed shared current perspective (leave-taking ritual). The rising tone choice reflects the speaker's desire to have this perspective confirmed. We can demonstrate this assumption even more clearly if, in fact, the proposed shared perspective is incorrect. For example, if the hearer says "Oh no, I'm just looking for my ID card in my bag and coat," the speaker may then overtly note their incorrect assumption by responding with something like "Oh, ok, it just looked like you were packing your bag."

In B, the speaker is certain that the hearer is leaving and is asking for information rather than confirmation. Because the speaker is requesting new information, this is communicated using a falling tone. Cheng, Greaves, & Warren (2008) describe this tonal opposition as pragmatically based—the difference between finding out (indicated by a falling tone) and making sure (indicated by a rising tone).

If it is indeed the case that pragmatic meaning as opposed to syntactic structure underlies tone choice in questions, it should be possible (and in fact, probable) that different question types will occur with both falling and rising tones depending on the communicative intent of the speaker. Two such examples (based on Brazil, 1997) are shown:

Example 1

A: I can't find my book.

B: // WHAT'S it ↘CALLED//

A: I can't find my book.

B: // WHAT'S it ↗CALLED//

SF 4.3

In Example 1, the speaker tells the hearer that s/he has lost a book. The hearer then asks for the title of the book and can choose either a rising or falling tone on the *wh-* question. Choice of a falling tone on the *wh-* question suggests a meaning of something like "I don't know what book you are talking about; tell me the title." It suggests that the speaker is requesting new information. Choice of a rising tone on the wh- question, however, suggests a meaning of something like "I think I know what book you are looking for; confirm the title." In this case, there is an assumption on the part of the speaker that this information may already be shared knowledge between the speaker and hearer.

We can conduct a similar exercise with yes-no questions. Example 2 is set in a doctor's office and imagines a query from the doctor that would appear as part of the doctor-patient interview:

Example 2

A: // do you feel ↗ANxious//

B: // do you feel ↘ANxious//

SF 4.4

In the first case, the doctor's choice of a rising tone suggests a meaning of something like "Based on your other responses, I think this seems like a reasonable perspective and something that I can assume is shared information. Please confirm that this is a correct assumption." In the second case, the choice of a falling tone suggests a meaning of "This is one question in a list of questions that I want to ask you. I am asking you for this new piece of information, and I have no specific expectations."

As a result of the differing communicative value of the tone choices themselves, Brazil suggests that yes-no questions may more commonly imply shared knowledge (rising tones) and *wh-* questions more commonly request new information (falling tones), thus accounting for the correlation that has been noted. Because this correlation is based on pragmatic assumptions rather than grammatical structure, any question, regardless of syntactic structure, can be uttered with any tone choice.

This discussion demonstrates the increased explanatory power of intonation choices if we move away from grammatical structure and toward a discourse-pragmatic framework. The role of tone choice in additional discourse contexts is discussed in Chapter 6.

4.3. The Function of the Level Tone

The final tone, the "neutral" or "o" tone (o = ➜) is realized as either a sustained level pitch or a tone with a slightly rising pitch. This is a unique tonal cue within the five choices because, unlike the rising and falling tones, it does not mark information as either known or unknown but as outside the communicative value of the message. The interactive context between the speaker and hearer is suspended, and this allows the speaker to signal that s/he is temporarily withdrawing from marking informative content. Generally speaking, this is not something that a speaker would typically want to do; however, there are discourse contexts in which a more neutral, level tone can be anticipated. Both Brazil (1997) and Crystal (1969) suggest that it is often used with semi-ritualized or routinized language behavior such as giving directives (close your ➜BOOKS, put down your ➜ PENS) or in choral repetition (our ➜ FAther// who art in ➜ HEAven//). Cheng, Greaves, and Warren (2008, p. 134) describe a similar usage in routinized utterances used by workers in service encounter interactions:

//➜ THANKS//

//my ➜PLEAsure//

//➜ THANK you//

//➜ oKAY//

Because it highlights a withdrawal from the ongoing interaction between speaker and hearer, the level tone can also be used by the speaker as a strategic device to signal to the hearer that the speaker is temporarily withholding their opinion. The next example (adapted from Hewings & Goldstein, 1998, p. 107) features this usage when A shows B a dress that she has tried on at the store:

    A: // What do you ➘THINK?//

    B: // ➔WELL…//

    A: // It's NOT a good ➘COlor//

    B: // I preferred the ➘BLUE//

SF 4.5

When A asks for B's opinion, rather than indicate unmitigated disagreement such as stating something like "it looks horrible," B uses a neutral tone (➔WELL) to imply a problem. A then responds to the underlying communicative value of the neutral tone and, using a falling tone, asserts that she thinks that the color is not right. This confirms to B that A agrees with her, and she then asserts *her* truthful opinion that she preferred an earlier choice. Müller (1996, p. 133) describes the neutral tone as a kind of **prosodic mitigating device,** or as "short tokens, long prosody." A great deal of information can be carried in this one particular tone choice that speaker-hearers from the same speech community understand as part of their tacit knowledge of social interaction.

Finally, the level tone commonly occurs in places where the speaker may have momentary problems with linguistic coding—for example, searching for a word, or stumbling over a word. This often causes the speaker to hesitate, which causes a temporary withdrawal by the speaker from the informative content of the discourse and is frequently marked with a filled pause such as *um* or *uh*. This is a typical feature of spontaneous speech in which we momentarily concentrate on what we are going to say rather than how it might fit into the world-view of the hearer. Unplanned or partially planned discourse is often replete with pause fillers and other kinds of hesitation markers, which are frequently uttered in a level tone:

// ➔ I// ➔ i HAVE er// ➔ ER// ➔ I// I mean you ➔KNOW// ➔ I// ➔ I//
➔ I// i REALly LIKE you know the➔ MEdical// ➘ PEOple//

(Cheng, Greaves, and Warren, 2008, p. 139)

4.4. Tonal Composition

Tonal composition describes the pattern of tone choices that typically occur in a particular discourse genre (Tench, 1996). For example, one of the ways in which we recognize the difference between a news broadcast and a classroom lecture is a speaker's typical tonal patterns as well as other conventionalized syntactic and lexical expressions. As an example, Pickering (2001) examined the tonal composition of teaching presentations from STEM classes taught by university teaching assistants in the US. In general, these presentations had 60 percent falling tones, 30 percent rising tones, and 10 percent level tones, which reflects the nature of the genre. Teachers are usually primarily concerned with communicating new informational content (hence the predominance of falling tones) and also demonstrating how this new information can be integrated with what students already know (hence a number of rising tones). Neutral tone choices were scattered throughout the presentations when teachers gave formulaic instructions, read information from a textbook or were momentarily distracted by extra-linguistic concerns such as writing on the board (see also Chapter 6).

4.5. Summary and Pedagogical Implications

Two issues should be borne in mind when considering tone choice in naturally occurring moment-by-moment interaction. First, any interaction, even one between strangers, occurs in some specified context and in choosing a certain tone, the speaker specifies that context for the hearer. In other words, the speaker's tone choice projects a context or current state of understanding. As we have said before with regard to the systems in the model, there is no situation in which a speaker must make a particular choice. Rather, the system operates on the assumption that speakers make contributions that are designed to be understood by their hearer(s). But, of course, a speaker might decide to manipulate the system for strategic reasons of some kind. This kind of ambiguity is built into the system itself and can be useful, as we saw in the example of the use of the neutral tone to avoid statements of disagreement.

Second, while stipulating that these are contextualized choices, under speaker control and made on a moment-by-moment basis, it is also the case that much of our everyday language is formulaic. Idiomatic lexical expressions often carry prepackaged intonation contours in addition to the prepackaged prominence patterns noted in Chapter 3. A typical example is known as the **calling contour** and comprises the sing-song falling tone that is used to call someone inside: "// ◥JOHNny!//." Standard tonal patterns include listing information, reading phone numbers, and others. This aspect of the system runs side by side with the moment-by-moment choices speakers make within the discourse.

Research in ESL/EFL learner acquisition suggests that tone choice is not automatically acquired and that learners of English encounter difficulties in applying tone choices appropriately. Using Brazil's model to undertake her analysis, Pirt (1990) reports that Italian learners of English use falling tones at boundaries between related propositions rather than rising or level tones. Hewings (1995) also found a preference for the use of falling tones in the discourse of advanced L2 learners from Korea, Greece, and Indonesia. Using the AM intonation model, Wennerstrom (1994, 1997) shows that Japanese, Thai, and Chinese speakers tended to use falling tones between related propositions where speaker-hearers of Traditional Englishes would expect rising tones. My own research shows that intermediate learners typically exhibit these characteristics:

- ◆ an overuse of falling tones accompanied by some level tones, which can contribute to learner being perceived as unfriendly or unengaged

- ◆ an exclusive use of one of the five tones regardless of the context of the interaction (e.g., overuse of falling tones between related propositions), which can contribute to misunderstanding of speaker intent by the hearer

- ◆ a lack of a sustained final tonal movement of any kind to mark the tonic syllable, which can contribute to confusion regarding prominence patterns and tone unit structure for the hearer.

As noted in Chapter 3, there is no reason to assume that learners will use tones correctly with no pedagogical intervention; in fact, the research suggests that all learners, regardless of their first language will face challenges with learning the tonal repertoire. It is important to bear in mind, however, that not every choice is equally weighted. Just as we would approach segmental instruction with a given learner by prioritizing those issues that most inhibit intelligibility, we can address the aspects of the tonal system that seem most likely to negatively impact communicative intent.

4.6. Check Your Learning

1. Why is it more productive to think of the rising and falling tonal opposition in discourse-pragmatic terms than in strictly grammatical terms?

2. Can you summarize the pragmatic meanings of the three major tone choices: falling (including rise-fall), rising (including fall-rise), and level?

3. Why is tonal composition an important feature of discourse genre?

4.7. Activities

1. Consider the popular game Twenty Questions in which someone has to guess which historical figure their partner is by asking only yes-no questions. Start playing the game with a partner and vary your final choices (rising or falling) on your questions—//ARE you ↘DEAD?// vs. //ARE you ↗DEAD?// Do both intonation choices sound okay?

2. One kind of question known as an **echo question** always appears with a rising tone. Based on the pragmatic meanings of the tones, think about why this would be the case.

3. Crystal & Davy (1969) identified the different prosodic characteristics of a number of discourse genres. For example, they noted that conversational speech tends to have short tone units (1–5 words), speaking a prayer aloud shows a high frequency of level tones, and that sports commentaries had much longer tone units (up to 10 words) and mainly level and falling tone choices. Pick a discourse genre (e.g., broadcast news, political speeches, read-aloud technical prose, dramatic dialogue) and find an example you can listen to on Youtube or a similar site. What can you say about the typical tonal composition of the genre?[1]

---

[1]This activity is based on Johns-Lewis (1986).

Chapter 5

Using Your Voice's Pitch Range: Key and Termination

This chapter presents the last of the systems in Brazil's model—**key** and **termination**—or high, mid, and low **pitch level** contrasts on two prominent syllables.

The system of key and termination, or what we can call the linguistically significant meaning of pitch range, is perhaps the least familiar part of the system for most teachers and students because of the difficulty in understanding what is meant by high, mid, and low levels of pitch.

One useful way to understand the concept is in physiological terms: Women usually have a higher pitch range than men, and the average pitch of children is higher still. Thus, what may be perceived as a high or low pitch varies by speaker. Yet research shows us that listeners are able to predict where a particular pitch may appear in a speaker's range when given enough context (Wong & Diehl, 2003). This is termed **speaker normalization** and, although the underlying processes are not yet completely understood, it is clear that listeners can distinguish linguistically significant differences in range (Honorof & Whalen, 2005).

Within Brazil's model, key is realized on the first prominent syllable in the tone unit and termination is realized on the last prominent syllable. As such, they form the left and right boundary edges of the tonic segment.

5.1. Key: Left Edge Boundary Pitch

Key choice is realized on the **onset syllable,** which is the first prominent syllable in the tonic segment. It is described using a three-term system of pitch height: high (⇑), mid (⇒) and low (⇓). Each choice has a particular

56

communicative value. The possible key choices of one example are summarized in Figure 5.1.

In Example 1, notice the mid key choice:

Example 1

👂📢 // she ⇨TOOK the exam and <u>FAILED</u>//
SF 5.1

Two important information choices are indicated by the speaker in the tone unit on the prominent syllables *took* and *failed*. This assumes a context in which the hearer knows that a discussion of the exam has already taken place because the word *exam* is not marked as prominent. The mid key choice on *took* carries an additive value, meaning that its communicative value is simply to impart the information with no additional commentary by the speaker. It denotes a straightforward expansion or enlargement of the information and can represent a meaning as something like "We were talking about the exam; now I'm reporting that she took the exam."

Contrast this with Example 2:

Example 2

👂📢 // she ⇧TOOK the exam and <u>FAILED</u>//
SF 5.2

Here the choice of high key on *took* denotes the information as contrastive, particularized, or adjudicating in some way in relation to the surrounding information and/or expectation. In this case, the contrastive value of the high key changes the communicative value to something like "We were talking about the exam; now I'm going to surprise you by telling you that she actually TOOK the exam!"

Figure 5.1.   Summary of Key Pitch Choices on the Onset Syllable

⇧TOOK
// she ⇨TOOK the exam and <u>FAILED</u> //
⇩TOOK

Finally, the speaker may choose a low key choice as shown in Example 3:

Example 3

◖(⊪ // she ⇩TOOK the exam and <u>FAILED</u>//
SF 5.3

Here the taking of the exam is something expected or of equative value with any previous understandings between speaker and hearer and can be expressed as "We were talking about the exam and, as you would expect, I'm now reporting that, of course, she took the exam."

5.2. Termination: Right Edge Boundary Pitch

Termination choice is realized on the final **tonic syllable.** It is described using the same three-term system as key and encompasses the same communicative values.

The same examples and context (see Figure 5.2) can also show the effect of termination choices. The mid termination choice, where a discussion of the exam has already taken place, is shown in Example 4:

Example 4

◖(⊪ // she TOOK the exam and ⇨<u>FAILED</u>//
SF 5.4

This mid pitch level choice on *failed* carries the same additive value as the mid key choice, and the meaning is something like "I'm reporting that she took the exam, and she failed the exam." Similarly, Example 5 shows a high termi-

Figure 5.2.   Summary of Termination Choices on the Tonic Syllable

⇧<u>FAILED</u>
//she TOOK the exam and ⇨ <u>FAILED</u> //
⇩ <u>FAILED</u>

nation on *failed,* which carries a contrastive value and means something like "I'm reporting that she took the exam and that, contrary to what you probably expected to hear, she did not pass it."

Example 5

(ᗩ)⑴ // she TOOK the exam and ⇧<u>FAILED</u>//
SF 5.5

Finally, the low termination choice shown in Example 6 carries a reformulative value and denotes the failure of the exam as something expected. It means "I'm reporting that she took the exam, and as you would expect from what you know of her, you will assume that taking it resulted in failing it."

Example 6

(ᗩ)⑴ // she TOOK the exam and ⇩<u>FAILED</u>//
SF 5.6

The separate choices of key and termination allow speakers to indicate highly nuanced communicative values within one tone unit if they choose to do so. Note that Example 7 shows a mid key and a high termination:

Example 7

(ᗩ)⑴ // she ⇨TOOK the exam and ⇧<u>FAILED</u>//
SF 5.7

This combination means something like "We are talking about the exam. I'm reporting that she took the exam but, surprisingly, she failed the exam."

Alternatively, speakers may choose to make only one syllable in the tone unit prominent (think for example of the minimal tone unit //<u>DUDE</u>// shown in Chapter 3). In this case, both key and termination are realized on the same tonic syllable, which forms the tonic segment and which is why they have equivalent communicative values.

In conversational interaction, key and termination choices allow the speaker to project certain assumptions or expected reactions toward the hearer (similar to the way in which a speaker can project disagreement through the use of a level, neutral tone.) The short exchange shown was heard on a college campus between two female students:

𝄞⁣ A: // it wasn't ⇑MY fault// ⇑WAS it//

  B: // ⇑ NO// of ⇑COURSE it ⇒WASn't// definitely ⇓NOT//

SF 5.8

Speaker A makes her request using a high contrastive key and termination that means "Tell me, was it or wasn't my fault?" Speaker B responds with a matching high key and termination choice on no, which means "I understand that you are asking me to make a decision between yes and no." A final low termination reformulation on *not* uttered by Speaker B closes the interaction and repeats her previous assertion that it was not Speaker A's fault.

As we demonstrated with recognizing prominence in Chapter 3 (see Figure 3.1, Dialogue 1), it can sometimes be easier to understand the tacit assumptions regarding the pragmatic meaning of these choices when norms are violated. The next interaction occurred between a Chinese learner of English (an international teaching assistant) who was teaching a chemistry class in a North American classroom and one of his North American students:

𝄞⁣ ITA: // ⇑WHAT'S the ⇒SEcond step//

  Student: // ⇒it dePENDS// ⇒you might have to do a
                   soLUtion test for poTAssium//

  ITA: // ⇑diRECTly then// ⇑HERE//

  Student: (Silent pause, flat pitch) //➔YEAH//

SF 5.9

The ITA asks the question, "What's the second step?" The student responds that it would depend on the previous findings and may involve a solution test. The teacher's response, "directly then? Here?" is spoken in a high contrastive key. Within this classroom context, the student is unsure how to interpret these choices which, from the student's perspective, means "Tell me, do you have to do a solution test at this time or don't you?" The student is surprised by the unusual "interrogation" style of the questioning, and his discomfort is evident in his answer, which is given hesitantly with a flat tone.

A more typical example of key and termination use in classroom interaction is shown between a teacher (T) and student (S) (both native speakers of General American English) in a similar chemistry lab:

⌒ᵢₗ T: // any ⇨su<u>GGES</u>tions//

    S: // ⇒p<u>H</u>//

    T: // ⇒p<u>H</u>// ⇨we'll HAVE to do that ⇨e<u>VENT</u>ually//
           but it's ⇨BEST to keep that off to the ⇓<u>END</u>//

SF 5.10

The teacher is asking the students for suggestions as to the next step in a chemical analysis that the students are about to perform. The student responds by suggesting that a test for *pH* value should come next. The teacher produces a highly mitigated response to the incorrect suggestion in line with the *"yes, but"* approach that teachers commonly take in North American classrooms. He notes that the students will indeed have to do that test but that it is *best to keep that off to the end.* His mid key and termination choices, which suggest agreement rather than disagreement, are an important part of the mitigation, but the final low termination he uses on the word *end* clearly indicates to the students that this suggestion is incorrect. In comparison to the first example, which was disorienting for the student, this is a clear but encouraging response by the teacher to the student.

As briefly noted in Chapter 2, key and termination also play a crucial role in the structure of speech-based units larger than the tone unit and in the cueing of the opening and closing of interactions. The left and right edge boundaries mark the beginning and end of the tonic segment. As such, they also provide information as to how one tonic segment fits in with those around it. For example, a mid termination may indicate a continuation of a telling increment, whereas a low termination may signal turn completion. This allows us to posit the creation of larger phonological units of organization both within the discourse of one speaker, called **pitch paragraphing**, and between speakers, called **pitch concord**.

5.3. Structure and Function of Pitch-Defined Paragraphs

As we noted in Chapter 3, it can be useful to equate unit division in the speech stream to that in written text as long as we remain flexible with the analogy. Thus, we can think of pitch-defined paragraphs as analogous to written paragraphs in the sense that both typically deal with a single topic or idea. Once again, the literature can be confusing. Different analytical approaches to spoken discourse have proposed this larger unit, but they have labeled and defined it differently. Speech paragraphs have been variously termed as major and minor paratones (Yule, 1980), pitch sequences (Brazil, 1997), sequence chains (Barr, 1990), phonological paragraphs (Tench, 1996) and major tone groups (Wichmann, 2000). Although criteria for their identification vary, there are a number of commonalities between them.

With regard to the structure of pitch paragraphs, analysts agree that the boundaries of these units are produced and interpreted using phonetic cues. The most prominent cues include a high pitch onset (high key) with an accelerated rate and volume and a low pitch close (low termination) possibly accompanied by a drop in volume and narrowing of the pitch range. Within the unit itself, researchers suggest that there will be a gradual descent in pitch from the first to the final paragraph (Tench, 1996) accompanied by longer pauses at boundaries, followed by a pitch reset to mark the beginning of the next speech paragraph. The height of the pitch reset will also gradually decline across a series of speech paragraphs within a single text. This is visualized in Figure 5.3.

Within Brazil's model, pitch paragraphs are termed **pitch sequences**, and as with all the systems in the model, the criteria for their recognition are the systematic pitch choices made by the speaker. Other criteria such as pausing, volume changes, or speech rate changes frequently co-occur. Key and termina-

Figure 5.3. Example of the Use of Key in Speech Paragraphs

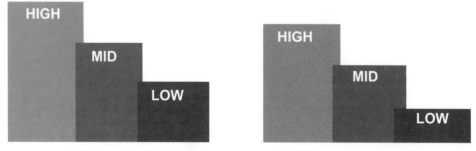

tion choices within a tone unit follow a stepwise pattern—for example, high to mid and mid to low rather than high to low. Thus a pitch sequence is a stretch of consecutive tone units that fall between two low termination choices.

The function of speech paragraphs is directly connected to the expression of topic structure. A speaker is likely to use a high pitch to initiate a new topic, a mid pitch at points of continuing a topic, and a low pitch for the closing of the topic, and also for any **asides** or digressions away from the topic. Some have suggested that the high pitch onset will coincide with a **topic statement** and that pitch level changes within the paragraph may correlate with **sub-topics** or "levels of embedding of a topic" (Wichmann, 2000, p. 130). This is exemplified here, adapted from Donna (2000):

⟲⟨⟨ ⇑LET'S look at the competition. Our main competitor—Benton—entered the market 10 years later than us. But since then, they have grown more rapidly and are now the biggest in terms of market share. Why? Their products are better, sold at lower prices, and presented more attractively.⇓

⇑NOW, our SEcond major competitor is Zecron. They entered the market at the same time as us. They have a lower market share than us and their products are sold at slightly higher prices. However, their annual return shows greater productivity.⇓

⇑The LAST major competitor is Mansell. They have a much smaller market share, but their products are sold at the top end of the market at much higher prices. As a result, they achieve the best profitability of the four companies with a much lower turnover.⇓

⇑SO, what can we say about our own position?

SF 5.11

Pitch sequence structure can also be shared between and among speakers. We saw an example of this in Chapter 2 when we looked at key and termination choices in a teacher-student initiation-response-feedback (IRF) interaction:

⟲⟨⟨ T: //⇒WHAT'S the final ⇒<u>ANS</u>wer//

S: //⇒ <u>TWELVE</u> //

T: //⇒TWELVE ⇓<u>GOOD</u>//

SF 5.12

Following the teacher's question using a mid key and termination choice, the student responds with a mid termination continuation on the answer *twelve*. This allows the teacher to respond with a mid agreement key and then close the pitch sequence with a low termination on the evaluation *good*.

5.4. Pitch Concord

The first pitch range pattern, pitch sequences, occurs within the discourse of one speaker. The second occurs exclusively between and among speakers. **Pitch concord** describes conversationalists' use of key and termination as a cue or signal of their agreement or disagreement with a previous speaker. This feature of pitch range interaction has also been described in different ways in the literature. Anderson (1990) calls it "a preferential relationship holding between pitch level choices in adjacent utterances" (p. 106); Couper-Kuhlen (1996) refers to it as melodic matching and Szczepek Reed (2006) as prosodic alignment or prosodic matching between speakers. In all cases, it describes a preference for a second speaker to use an initial pitch choice, in terms of relative pitch height, that matches the final pitch choice of the first speaker as one way to express agreement as with the first speaker. Conversely, the expression of disagreement by a second speaker may be signaled by a mismatch of this pitch choice. This is termed **concord-breaking,** or prosodic non-matching, and is signaled by the use of a significantly higher or lower pitch by the second speaker. In other words, pitch concord occurs between speakers when a second speaker echoes the termination choice of the previous speaker in his/her selection of key or key/termination, as shown in these examples:

Example 8

👂 A: // do you ⇒under<u>STAND</u>//

    B: // ⇒ <u>YES</u>/

Example 9

    A: // do you ⇑under<u>STAND</u>//

    B: // ⇑ <u>YES</u>//

SF 5.13

In Example 8, the use of mid termination by Speaker A is interpreted not only as a request for a decision, but also as an invitation for B to confirm A's assumption, which means "I think you understand." Speaker B supplies this expected concurrence with a mid key that means "Yes, I do understand." In Example 9, on the other hand, the use of the high pitch termination by Speaker A means "Tell me, do you or do you not understand?" and Speaker B's matching high response expresses "Yes, there is no question of me not understanding."

In this sense, pitch concord is one way in which speakers of Traditional Englishes can show their affiliation with each other. The next interaction was collected by a graduate student at her sorority house. We can see A and B affiliating with each other through their matching high and mid key and termination choices at their leave-taking:

⟨⟩ A: // I've gotta ⇧<u>RUN</u>// It's so good ⇧<u>MEET</u>ing you Mark//

 B: // It's ⇧<u>NICE</u> to meet ⇧<u>YOU</u>//

 A: // ⇧ <u>YEAH</u>// and ⇧<u>THANKS</u> for the ⇒<u>CHOC</u>olate//

 B: // yeah you're ⇒<u>WEL</u>come//

 A: // ⇒ <u>THANK</u> you//[1]

SF 5.14

As noted in Chapter 4, in terms of tone choice, there is no absolute requirement that a speaker must obey the concord norm. In fact, the system can be manipulated to signal disagreement either directly or indirectly. We saw this previously in our "short tokens, long prosody" delay devices that are realized using a neutral tone such as //➔ <u>WELL</u>//. In addition to the neutral level tone on this "dummy" item, the speaker may further mitigate upcoming disagreement by using a mid termination choice prior to choosing a concord-breaking pitch choice:

⟨⟩ A: // I ⇒<u>COULD</u>n't go//⇒<u>COULD</u> I//

 B: // ⇒ <u>WELL</u>// ⇧ <u>YES</u> actually// I think you ⇧<u>COULD</u>//

SF 5.15

---

[1]With thanks to Melissa Chase for these data.

Here the direct disagreement given in a high, contrastive key/termination, is prefaced by the mid key/termination on the discourse marker *well*. Concord-breaking that signals direct disagreement is often realized by a number of co-occurring phonetic features, such as raised pitch or volume, and can also be accompanied by additional discourse cues such as interrupting another speaker's turn. In all cases, Anderson (1990) notes that in Traditional Englishes, "concord-breaking will not pass unobserved but be taken as meaningful by speakers" (p. 107).

5.5. Question Types and Key Choice

Because of the prevalence of grammatical question types in intonation instruction materials for EFL/ESL, we will focus briefly here on key/termination choice and question types. Within the Brazil discourse model presented, the greater number of oppositions are motivated by the ways in which key or key plus termination can further pinpoint the pragmatic intent of the speaker. For example, a speaker may use a falling or rising tone with a high, mid, or low key, and choices will be based on the local context. Using some of the examples from Chapter 4 may help. As a reminder, Example 10 shows a rising tone choice in a yes-no question, which means something like "It looks like you are leaving. Can you confirm that I am correct?" Example 11 shows the same rising tone with the addition of a high termination.

Example 10

👂⁽ⁱⁱ // ↗Are you <u>LEAV</u>ing//

Example 11

      // ↗ are you ⇑<u>LEAV</u>ing//
SF 5.16

The high termination adds a contrastive or particularized meaning that means something like "It looks like you are leaving but that is very unexpected; can you confirm that I am correct?" A mid termination, on the other hand, // ↗ are you ⇒<u>LEAV</u>ing// does not carry this additional contrastive value.

Similar communicative values apply in *wh-* questions. The mid key termination in Example 12 expresses "I can see that you are leaving but I don't know why so please tell me." In Example 13, the high termination with the falling tone carries an additional sense of improbability, which means something like "I can see that you leaving but I don't know why and I'm very surprised that you would do that so please tell me why."

Example 12

☊⟮⟮ // ↘WHY are you ⇨<u>LEAV</u>ing//

Example 13

// ↘ why are you ⇧<u>LEAV</u>ing//

SF 5.17

5.6. Summary and Pedagogical Implications

This chapter has focused on the function of pitch height as opposed to pitch movement. Although it is often underutilized in pedagogical materials, it has been successfully used to systematically describe contrastive pitch heights in Traditional Englishes, and how these might vary in New and Emerging varieties of English as well as in learner discourse. Key and termination is also the system that has come under the strongest criticism from other intonation researchers (interested readers might like to look at Gussenhoven, 1983, or Jassem & Demnko, 1986). Detractors have noted that it is clear that for any given speaker, an infinite number of absolute pitch levels may be identified. In addition, a certain amount of flexibility needs to remain within the system. Pitch changes within a single speaker are conditioned by both the time of the utterance, which causes a physical declination or lowering of the voice over the length of the utterance, and position of the utterance in the discourse, which results in an expansion or flattening of the intonation contour near the beginning and ends of intonation units (Beckman, 1997; Levelt, 1989).

If we move away from these primarily phonetic concerns, however, it is possible to identify the minimally fixed framework, or voice range of a given speaker (Couper-Kuhlen, 1986) and from this, identify pitch choices that are appreciably higher than or lower than preceding key and termination choices within a speaker's range. Based on these choices it has been possible for both intonologists and teaching specialists to identify beginnings, middles, and ends based on systematic pitch choices in spoken discourse (Gorsuch et al., 2010; Wichmann, 2000).

Although our focus in this chapter has been on the role of key and termination in social and informational convergence, pitch level changes also occur due to emotional affect. For example, speakers may use an extra-high pitch when they are angry, excited, or frightened. Although we can make some general statements regarding extra-high pitch, it is difficult to isolate the function of pitch level specifically in these contexts as perceptions of affect are derived from a number of linguistic and paralinguistic features including gestures, eye-gaze, and facial expressions.

Pitch level choices are also associated with indexical or sociocultural functions. There have been a number of studies examining a possible correlation between perceptions of sexuality and pitch range (see Levon, 2006, for a summary). Van Bezooijen (1995) found that Japanese women had a preference for using a higher pitch than Dutch women and suggests that this is a vocal device associated with feminine attributes within a Japanese cultural context. At the opposite end of the pitch range, mainstream media in the U.S. is replete with discussion of the new trend toward creaky voice or vocal fry among young women in the U.S. in which the frequency of voice vibrations is reduced resulting in a low "creak" in the voice.

Although some research has been conducted in the area of L2 learners and key and termination, it has been quite limited. Investigation of monologues both inside and outside the classroom show that pitch sequence structure is hampered by an overall lack of pitch range in non-native speaker presentations. In data that I presented in 2004, there was a significant difference between native and non-native speaker pitch ranges in similar classroom contexts. The overall pitch range of teaching presentations given by native speakers was between 50 and 250 hertz (the unit of measurement used to calculate pitch (HZ)). In contrast, non-native speakers varied their pitch range between only 100 and 200 HZ, and their pitch levels were more variable and less systematic. Mennen (1999) reported similar results in her data and suggests that the significantly narrower pitch range demonstrated by many L2 speakers may be related to a lack of confidence in the new language. It is also the case that pedagogical literature is virtually silent on the subject of pitch paragraphing, and a lack of focus on this area in teaching contexts may also contribute to the problem.

With regard to pitch phenomena in conversation, it seems that ELLs do not necessarily acquire this skill early in their production. Pickering & Levis (2002) found that lower-proficiency ELLs were less able to manipulate pitch range patterns in interaction and this aspect of prosodic production appeared to develop over time. Koester (1990) found that a lack of pitch concord between German learners of English (the use of a low termination where a mid termination was expected) prompted the first speaker to need to confirm their partner's agreement. In a study of L2 prosody, Anderson (1990) reports an interaction between an English speaker and a Dutch speaker of English in which high pitch choices by the nonnative speaker project conflict and result in a failed interaction.

There has also been some work on the differences between typical pitch ranges in different languages and how that may contribute to L2 production. Mennen (2007) found significant differences in pitch range characteristics between native English speakers and German speakers of English. She suggests that German exhibits a narrower pitch range than English overall, thus German speakers may transfer this characteristic to English, which may result in unintentional concord breaking by L2 speakers. Interestingly, O'Brien (2014) found that American English learners of German also produced their German using a wider pitch range than native speakers thus supporting Mennen's conclusions.

At least one study of the fundamental frequency (F0) in Arabic learners of English (Abu-Al-Makarem and Petrosino, 2007) has observed that the mean fundamental frequency for spontaneous speech samples of Arabic speakers was "significantly higher" than for Euro-American, African-American, and Polish samples (p. 576), and that "young Arab men speak generally louder than Euro-American men" (p. 579). Both prosodic features, pitch and volume, could be perceived to be an intentional form of concord breaking in interactions with speakers of Traditional Englishes.

5.7. Check Your Learning

1. What are the differences between key and termination?

2. How do we recognize the boundaries of pitch sequences?

3. How might speakers show that they agree with each other using pitch level choices?

5.8. Activities

1. Couper-Kuhlen (2001) notes that speakers will often use a high key onset as a strategic resource to insert a new topic into an interaction. Based on the pragmatic values associated with key choices, why might this be the case?

2. The current fashion of young U.S. women to use creaky voice has been both lauded and criticized in the media. A commentator on *Slate*'s language podcast called the trend "annoying" and "repulsive."[2] On the other hand, Gabriel Arana (2013) describes such reactions as typical in response to the "linguistic ingenuity" of young women by NORMs (non-mobile, older, rural males). Listen to this short clip about vocal fry on YouTube (https://www.youtube.com/watch?v=Ff1JByylQU0) and discuss your reactions to this trend.

3. The concepts of key and termination allow us to divide spoken texts into pitch paragraphs in a principled way. Take a sample spoken text (examples can be found on the IDEA dialects archive found at www.dialectsarchive.com) and decide where you think pitch paragraphs would be marked.

[2]From: www.slate.com/articles/podcasts/lexicon_valley/2013/01/lexicon_valley_on_creaky_voice_or_vocal_fry_in_young_american_women.html

Chapter 6

The Social Life of Intonation[1]

It is no coincidence that the culture of emoji has flourished alongside the increased use of text-based communication using phones and computers. An emoji showing a face with a winking eye and tongue stuck out might be used to indicate that whatever was just written should not be taken seriously but as a joke. This is something that a speaker could show in a number of different ways in face-to-face interaction, and particularly in their intonation, as Vyv Evans notes in his OxfordWords blog of April 16, 2016: "For most people, and most of the time, emojis are used to add a personal voice to digital text . . . . In this it [can sometimes] fulfill a communicative value similar to intonation in a spoken language."

Intonation choices play a significant role in communicating to others how we want to be understood (e.g., teasing them or scolding them) and also how we expect to be treated. This is particularly true in **asymmetrical interactions** in which there is some kind of important power differential between speakers (e.g., doctor and patient or teacher and student). This chapter looks at how the tone system is leveraged by speakers of Traditional Englishes to express some of these nuances of meaning.

---

[1] The phrase—*the social life of intonation*—was first used by Don Rubin in his plenary at the 3rd Annual PSLLT Conference in 2011.

6.1. Revisiting Tone Choice

Chapter 4 introduced the overall pragmatic functions of falling tones (fall **↘**, rise-fall **↗↘**) and rising tones (rise **↗**, fall-rise **↘↗**), but it did not distinguish between types of falls and rises. Brazil argues that the pragmatic difference between these tone types is the communicative value they project based on the social relationship or role relationships between speakers. Participants claiming control or dominance at any given time in the interaction can employ the **dominant** version of each tone (the **rise-fall ↗↘** and the **rise↗**) as a cue to other participants that they are, at least temporarily, directing the interaction. The four tone choices are shown in Figure 6.1.

Brazil (1997) notes that "the local meaning of the '+' [or dominant] options of each type is often affected by very obscure considerations of conversational finesse" (p. 86). In other words, we should not interpret the notion of dominance too literally; this is illustrated here: When asked to help, a speaker may respond by using the non-dominant options of the rising and falling tones (a fall-rise and a fall), as shown in A or by the + options of rising and falling tones (rise and rise-fall) as shown in B:

A: // when I've finished what I'm
　　 ↘↗<u>DO</u>ing// I'll **↘**<u>HELP</u> you//

B: // when I've finished what I'm
　　 ↗<u>DO</u>ing// I'll **↗↘**<u>HELP</u> you//

SF 6.1

Figure 6.1. Four Falling and Rising Tone Choices

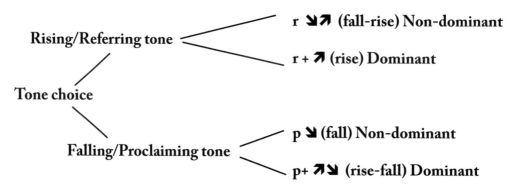

A projects an accommodating and helpful stance and means something like "Just hang on a minute, and I'll help you." In B, using the controlling or dominant choices projects a more forceful or exasperated stance and can be understood as something like "If you want me to help you, you'll have to wait." As Brazil notes, if this were an interaction between an adult and a child, the use of the + options in B by the child would be considered rude. Between two adults, the use of the + options may be heard as peremptory or as overly emphatic.

This perception is of course, very dependent on context and possibly power relationships. In the next example from Cheng, Greaves & Warren (2008, p. 151), a speaker in a televised discussion speaks authoritatively and holds the floor by using dominant rising tones as he lists problems that Hong Kong experienced in the 1960s:

> // we HAVE the ↗REfugees// the ↗RIots//
> the ↗WAter SHORtage// the ↘BANK runs//

It is also important to be clear that the label of dominance does not necessarily imply negativity or some kind of aggressive seizure of control by a speaker. Imagine a stranger stopping you in the street in your hometown to ask for directions. It is probable that you will use the dominant, rising tone in your response as though you are giving a series of commands, for example:

🎧 //you need to take the first ↗LEFT// go straight until the ↗STOP sign
//about a quarter of a ↗MIle// and then turn ↘RIGHT//

SF 6.2

In this situation, the dominant status is briefly conferred at this moment of this interaction. You can rightly claim control of the discourse as the person who is in possession of the needed information and, as such, you bear a greater responsibility for the discourse. Should the conversation continue onto other topics, the control may change to someone else.

The distinction between non-dominant and dominant tone choices is particularly significant when we consider asymmetrical interaction—that is, interaction in which the status of the participants is unequal. This type of communication is particularly common in **institutional talk** in which there is often differential distribution of knowledge and unequal allocation of participant rights (Drew & Heritage, 1992; Koshik, 2000; Schiffrin, 1994). The next section examines classroom discourse as an example of this kind of interaction.

6.2. Classroom Discourse

Classroom discourse is a prototypical example of asymmetrical interaction. The role relationships between the participants are clearly defined, and the style of speaking/interacting is one that everyone is very familiar with, as both teachers and students have "learned" the business of classroom interaction over time. It is the teacher's perogative as the person with the highter status to choose dominant tones. Use of the dominant tones by the clearly non-dominant participant (i.e., the student) would be perceived as openly rude or hostile.

Pickering's (2001) study revealed that teachers take advantage of their freedom to negotiate a more controlling stance. However, their tone choices also suggest that they are unwilling to project a message of total authoritarianism. It seems equally important to these speakers that they create a sense of community in the classroom, and this is achieved in part by tone choice. We can see how this works in the next example, in which a math teacher explains the last of three variables (r) that the students in the class need to understand an equation.

⌒⍾ // and r's what's ↘CALLED a ↘GROWTH constant// if r's
     ↘↗POsitive// the THING's getting ↘↗BIGger// ↗RIGHT//
SF 6.3

The falling tones in the first two tone units assert new information—"r is a growth constant." The next two tone units—"if r's positive, the thing's getting bigger, you're getting more money" are projected using non-dominant fall-rise tones. This is something that students should know from their real-world experience and is projected as shared knowledge. The communicative effect of these units can be understood as something like "I am telling you that r is called a growth constant. I assume that you understand, like me, that if r is positive, the element is increasing." The final unit comprises the **confirmation marker** *right* with a dominant rising tone. When these markers appear in the classroom, teachers frequently do not follow them with any wait time; in other words, they do not permit or expect students to verbally respond. These markers are not requests for affirmation from the students, but instead might be viewed as interactional devices used to project confirmation of their belief that there is shared knowledge. The use of the dominant rising tone puts additional pressure on the students to agree. Thus, the dominant rising tone is used by teachers to reaffirm their authority, while simultaneously emphasizing community. We can see a similar use of the dominant rising tone in this example where the teacher interrupts to remind the student to adhere to the time limit and finish up the presentation.

> // could you sort of WRAP it up with the next FIVE minutes or ↗ SO//
> ↗ PLEASE//
>
> (Cheng, Greaves, & Warren, 2008, p. 154)

The dominant falling tone (rise-fall ↗↘) is the least common tone choice across all discourse genres, including teaching discourse. As a falling tone, it carries the pragmatic value of an assertion or statement; additionally, there is a sense of the speaker intervening to assert control over the progress of the discourse. In the next example, the speaker realizes that there is a problem with the recording device being used and interrupts another speaker to stop the speaking in order to check the device:

> // JUST a Second ↗↘STOP//
>
> (Cheng, Greaves, & Warren, 2008, p. 156)

As noted above, teachers generally work toward a balance between being authoritative and creating a **positive affect** (Bailey, 1984) with their students. In the university teaching data discussed in Pickering (2001), the rise-fall tone was rarely used by North American teachers, and never used to interrupt students. However, in teaching contexts involving young children, we might anticipate its appearance. Brazil (1997) notes that if we want to get someone's attention—say a small child in a classroom—the teacher may initially use a falling tone to attract the child's attention (see A) and, if unsuccessful, follow it up with a dominant rise-fall tone with a probable increase in loudness, as shown in B:

🔊 A: // ↘PEter//...//↘STOP it//

    B: // ↗↘PEter//...//↗↘STOP it//

SF 6.4

6.3. Revisiting Tonal Composition

Chapter 4 showed how tone choices are an important feature of tonal composition; but now let's fill in more detail. In university STEM classes taught by General American English speakers, for example, the discourse comprised roughly 60 percent falling tones, 30 percent rising tones, and 10 percent level tones (Pickering, 2001). Let's now bring in the fact that teachers also distinguish between types of rising and falling tones. Non-dominant rising tones (↘↗) were used more frequently than their dominant counterparts (↗), and the latter were used for confirmation markers and other assertions of shared knowledge. Falling tones were almost exclusively non-dominant (↘), and dominant rise-fall tones (↗↘) were never used in one-on-one interaction with students.

Brazil describes this composition of mostly falling and rising tones as an example of **direct orientation** where the speaker makes tone choices for the benefit of the hearer. The teacher selects falling or rising tones based on an understanding of whether the information is world-changing for the student or is shared. Thus, the teacher's choices are directly oriented toward achieving a **state of convergence** with their students.

The tonal system also allows the speaker to make choices that project minimal involvement with the hearer and indicate a temporary withdrawal from the context of the interaction. This alternative selection of a combination of falling and level tones creates **oblique orientation,** or an orientation by the speaker toward the language sample itself and away from the hearer. The principal characteristics of an oblique orientation are the use of level and falling tones, often accompanied by multiple prominences. For example, a speaker may decide to use a familiar quotation such as "You can lead a horse to water, but you can't make him drink" or "He who hesitates is lost":

👂⑴ //you can LEAD a HORSE to →WAter// but you CAN'T MAKE him
     ↘DRINK//

     //HE who →HEsitates// is ↘LOST//

SF 6.5

An utterance presented in this manner can be understood as "These are not my words addressed particularly to you on this occasion; they are rather a routine performance whose appropriateness to our present situation we both recognize" (Brazil, 1997, p. 136).

Oblique orientation choices can be a characteristic feature of a particular speech event, such as a choral prayer or other liturgical events in which participants recite formulaic responses. They can also be the result of a temporary orientation within a directly oriented speech event. This temporary oblique orientation may be the result of speaker hesitation due to momentary problems with linguistic coding or because the speaker is reading out information and is focused solely on the language sample rather than the hearers. In the next example, a university physics lab presentation, the teacher follows his opening remarks "So you guys had problems with the prelab, right?" with a series of falling and level tones, indicating a temporary shift in his focus away from the students to reading the question directly from the textbook.

👂(ᵗᵉ // so you GUYS had ↘PROBlems// with the ↘PRElab// ↗ RIGHT// →AND// the FIRST question →WAS uh// QUEStion ↘ONE was// for the exAMple on pages four and ↘FIVE// FIND out →TORQUES// for an AXis at x equals ↘ZEro//

SF 6.6

As we might expect, university classroom discourse spoken by North American teachers overwhelmingly comprises a direct orientation (i.e., a co-occurring selection of rising and falling tones) so as to project maximum involvement with students. Teachers typically exploit the converging functions of rising tones to foster an interactive teaching style in the classroom. What we might think of as the "scolding" inflection that can be projected by a rise-fall tone is avoided, and a shift to an oblique orientation (i.e., a co-occurring selection of level and falling tones with multiple prominences) is usually temporary and the result of momentary distraction due to extra-linguistic concerns such as writing on the board, or the use of routinized or formulaic language use (like from a textbook).

The pedagogical implications section of this chapter will look at how these intonational characteristics may diverge in the teaching discourse of non-native, international teaching assistants (usually speakers of Emerging varieties of English) in a North American university context.

6.4. Summary and Pedagogical Implications

This chapter completed our discussion of the tone choice system focusing on the differences in the communicative value of the two different falling (fall and rise-fall) and rising (rise and fall-rise) tones. The dominant tones in each pair (rise-fall and rise) convey an additional sense of control, dominance or authority that is particularly evident in interactions between participants who are unequal in terms of power. This might be simply the difference between an adult and a child or a more complicated power differential between two adults.

The chapter has included a number of examples of teaching discourse between international teaching assistants (ITAs) and their students, and this is an important group of English language learners to focus on with regard to the pedagogical implications of more nuanced tone choices. The number of ITAs continues to increase in North American universities, and intercultural communication has become an integral part of academic life. A considerable body of work investigating the performance of ITAs in the classroom and the responses of their students has been undertaken, and it is well established that these interactions are highly vulnerable to misunderstandings and communication breakdowns. Researchers have suggested a number of ways in which ITAs might improve their rapport with their students including learning and using their first names, using inclusive pronouns such as 'we' rather than 'you', and making eye contact with the students (Myers, Zhong & Guan, 1998). However, intonation is rarely comprehensively addressed despite the considerable role it plays in hearers' perceptions.

Early studies showed that ITAs were not always aware of the variety of intonational cues they may need in the classroom, and that they were also uncomfortable in their ability to assess their meaning in the speech of their students (Hinofotis & Bailey, 1980; Tyler & Davies, 1990). Pickering (2001, 2004) showed that an overuse of falling tones and a compression of pitch range resulted in the projection of an oblique orientation in which ITAs appear to be disengaged or uninterested in their students. In part, this impression was created by a lack of rapport-building strategies between ITAs and students using the social convergence function of the rising tone. The significant difference in tonal composition between the two groups of teachers (NA TAs and ITAs) meant that the ITAs were not seen as building or exploiting common ground, but were being perceived rather as nonassimilated participants who were placing themselves outside the group. This occurred not only in the ITAs' presentations, but crucially, in teacher-student exchanges. For example, in cases where the students gave incorrect answers to teachers' questions, North American TAs typically exploited the choice of a slight rising tone to show that the students were wrong in order to mitigate disagreement with their students (see the "yes, but" strategy discussed in Chapter 4). ITAs, however, tended to use less mitigating intonation patterns such as abruptly falling tones, and thus their attempts to increase interactivity in the classroom often failed. ITAs are not infrequently perceived by their students as being uncooperative and lacking in empathy and as Lippi-Green (2012) notes with comments from students, "emotions on the matter of graduate student instructors in the classroom sometimes run very high" (p. 90):

> Of course it's hard to understand them, and of course I resent it. Why can't I get what I pay for, which is a teacher like me who talks to me in my own language that I can understand? (From a questionnaire distributed annually to incoming students in a linguistics course) (p. 91)

This research makes clear the need to include instruction in the pragmatic role of intonation for ESL learners involved in interaction with speakers of Traditional Englishes (see, for example, Gorsuch et al (2013) for a recent treatment). This is particularly important for speakers of Emerging Englishes who are engaged in **binding discourse** (Goffman, 1981)—that is, settings in which the hearers are "bound" by the result of the interaction. In the case of the university teaching discourse, for example, the students may feel that they have a considerable amount at stake because they will be graded by their ITAs. Training in intonation for speakers who are going to be engaged in similar English for Specific Purposes (ESP) settings such as the medical, legal, or business fields would also be advisable.

6.5. Check Your Learning

1. In what ways is the description of the particular types of rising (➚) and falling (➚➘) tones as dominant tones highly dependent on situational context?

2. Can you summarize the difference between a direct and oblique discourse orientation?

3. In what ways can tone choice contribute to inter-speaker cooperation both positively and negatively in the classroom?

6.6. Activities

1. The fact that the use of dominant tones by the clearly non-dominant participant (for example, a student) is likely to be perceived as inappropriate was discussed. This example was heard in a college classroom where the teacher was a Chinese ITA with limited language proficiency and apparently ambiguous dominant status. At one point, after several repetitive checks by the ITA on student comprehension, this exchange occurred:

   T: Does everyone understand? Are there any questions?

   S: //↗↘ NO// just go ↗↘ON// ↗↘ PLEASE//

   SF 6.7

   Despite the ostensibly polite lexical form, it was clear from the negative reactions of the observer and the other students in the class that this response was perceived as highly disrespectful. Why might the observers interpret the interaction this way based on the tone choice of the student?

2. Based on the description of tonal composition of university teaching discourse, consider the likely tonal composition of other speech events (e.g., a sermon, a poetry reading, a child reading out a story vs. an adult reading aloud a story).

3. The largest prosodic corpus currently in use is the Hong Kong Corpus of Spoken English (HKCSE), a two million–word corpus of naturally occurring discourse in which approximately half of the discourse is prosodically transcribed using Brazil's discourse intonation framework. The corpus comprises four sub-corpora: academic, business, conversation, and public. Speakers comprise both Hong Kong Chinese English speakers and speakers of English from a variety of (unspecified) Traditional Englishes including Australian, American and British English.

As part of their examination of the corpus, Cheng, Greaves, & Warren (2008, p. 157) investigated the distribution of the dominant rising tone (➚) across the sub-corpora. They looked specifically at the use of the dominant rise tone across different discourse types on a continuum. At one end of the continuum, the use of the rise tone is evenly spread between the discourse participants (i.e., 50:50 in two-party discourse), and at the other end, the use of the rise tone is monopolized by a dominant speaker (85:15). Table 6.1 shows this distribution (Cheng, Greaves, & Warren, 2008). Discuss why you think particular speech events appear where they do on the continuum.

Table 6.1. Distribution of Rising Tones in HKCSE

Distribution of rising tones	50:50	67:33	75:25	85:15	100:0
Speech events	conversations	service encounters	business meetings	academic supervisions	none

Source: Data from Cheng, Greaves, & Warren, 2008, p. 157.

Chapter 7

Variation between Traditional and New Varieties of English

"We judge others by actions; we judge ourselves by intentions."
                                                    —fortune cookie

Language is a very flexible tool. It can be used to tease, scold, argue, comfort, or placate. Speaker-hearers of any given speech community are excellent at figuring out which intention is meant, although they also occasionally get it wrong. **Intercultural communication** requires us to become experts in interpreting a new set of conventions and their associated intents. Some **linguistic cues** may no longer apply while others may mean something entirely different. When engaged in intercultural communication, speakers typically will try to infer intent using cues that are familiar to them. This is a particularly significant issue when we look at the role of intonation, a relational and informational cue that is so tacitly understood that it is difficult to recognize its role in guiding interpretations with regard to speaker intent.

For a language such as English, which comprises many different varieties spoken around the world, it can be additionally problematic when speakers from these different varieties interact. It is often easy in these situations to think that we are all using the same type of communication, which may vary slightly perhaps in its choices of vocabulary or idioms. In fact, the differences between varieties are far more substantive, particularly with regard to intonation choices. This chapter examines intercultural communication between speaker-hearers of Traditional and New Englishes. Recall that New Englishes comprise those varieties that resulted from colonization in Asia and Africa, which include Indian English, a number of West and East African varieties of English, Singaporean and Malaysian English, and a number of others. Examples of many of these can be found in the International Corpus of English at (http://www.ucl.ac.uk/english-usage/projects/ice.htm). This chapter focuses primarily on Indian English, which has been a longtime research interest of mine (Pickering, 1999; Pickering & Wiltshire, 2000), but also briefly on more recent research on Southeast Asian Englishes in Singapore, Malaysia, and the Philippines.

Although previous chapters divided the discourse intonation model into its component systems, Chapters 7–10 consider all systems together (because unit structure, prominence, tone, and key and termination choice are interlocking systems).

7.1. Different Communication Styles and the Linguistic Penalty

In 2006, Roberts and Campbell published a report for the Department for Work and Pensions in the U.K. in which they described the **linguistic penalty** faced by many transnationals who interview for jobs for which they are professionally qualified. They note that the linguistic penalty arises "not from a lack of fluency in English but [is] largely hidden [in] demands to talk in institutionally credible ways" (p. 13) and particularly, communicative styles that may be at odds with their interviewers:

> Different ethnic groups, whether they use English as their heritage language or not, may use culturally specific styles of communication which are different from local or standard English . . . . Differences include a range of rhetorical and self-presentational features [including] a range of paralinguistic features such as intonation and rhythm. (p. 24)

Chapter 1 featured an example of this kind of mismatch of intonational features between Indian English-speaking workers in a cafeteria and the Traditional English-speaking workers using the cafeteria who perceived them to be "surly and uncooperative." In that case, John Gumperz (1982) diagnosed an important difference in the use of tone between the two varieties that neither group was aware of but which lay at the heart of the misunderstanding. Roberts and Campbell's analysis is based on this early work by John Gumperz who showed that the way in which participants oriented themselves to each other depended on their ongoing interpretation of linguistic cues or devices present at all levels of the discourse structure, including patterns found in the grammar, lexicon, and prosody.

When producing and interpreting these devices, previous experience, derived from their shared linguistic and sociocultural background, is used, according to Gumperz. Over time, Gumperz says that these cues become tacit, convention-alized choices, and in normal interaction between members of the same speech community, discourse participants will implicitly assume a shared framework of production and interpretation. These cues are "rarely consciously noted and almost never talked about directly" (1982, p. 131).

This set of implicit assumptions on the part of speakers directly impacts interactional success in intercultural speech events. First, contrasting behaviors across speech communities may not be immediately evident because interpreta-tion rests on deeply rooted understandings that are not always easily retrieved by a member of a given speech community on a conscious, analytical level. Second, research shows us that participants are likely to assume a mutual understanding of discourse conventions and infer speaker intent within their own interpretive framework (Green, 1989). In this sense, we come to any interaction with a set of expectations that we have honed since childhood, and we are used to assum-ing that whomever we speak to will essentially mirror these behaviors. Thus, as the interaction proceeds, participants may find themselves drawing closer together or further apart based on whether their expectations are being met, although not making clear what those expectations are. And they are almost certainly unaware of the fleeting and tacit cues that may be accumulating and dominating their interpretation.

Gumperz was particularly interested in "the use of a different set of uncon-scious linguistic conventions (such as tone of voice) to emphasize, to signal logical connections and to indicate the significance of what is being said in terms of overall meaning and attitudes" (1982, p. 12). He specifically noted the vulnerability of intonational cues wherein miscues are often interpreted in attitudinal terms:

> A speaker is said to be unfriendly, impertinent or rude, uncooperative or fail to understand . . . miscommunication of this type in other words is regarded as a social faux pas and leads to misjudgments of the speaker's intent . . . it is not likely to be identified as mere linguistic error. (1982, p. 139)

What are these alternative cuing systems with regard to intonational systems in different varieties of English? And how might they affect interactional success between speakers?

7.2. Intonational Cues across Varieties of English

7.2.1 Indian English

As is typical in many New Englishes contexts, Indian English forms only one part of a network of linguistic relationships within and between speakers. Here, for example, is Pandit's (1979) description of a typical multilingual speaker in India:

> An Indian businessman lives in a suburb of Bombay. His mother tongue and home language is a dialect of Gujarati; in the market he uses a familiar variety of Marathi, the state language; at the railway station he speaks the pan-Indian lingua franca, Hindustani; the language of work is Kachi, the code of the spice trade; in the evening he will watch a film in Hindi or in English and listen to a cricket-match commentary on the radio in English. (cited in Jayaraj, Leelavathi, & Merlin, 2015)

In addition to the regular use of multiple languages, access to English education and ultimate proficiency in the language is not uniform across India. These inequities in the system have created a varietal continuum or a cline of bilingualism (Kachru, 1985, p. 70). This is also sometimes described as a **cline of proficiency** from the perspective of the perceived intelligibility of some Indian English speakers by hearers from other varieties. Despite this variation, research has demonstrated that there are a number of pan-Indian features (or General Indian English features) evident within the variety.

These General Indian English characteristics with regard to intonation structure will be discussed. Systematic differences between Indian English and Traditional Englishes are present in these areas: (1) phonetic realization of prominence; (2) differences in prominence patterns; (3) substitution of pitch register shifts for tonal movement; (4) sub-contours within expected tone units.

7.2.1.1 Phonetic Realization of Prominence

The feature of prominence is crucial in the identification of information structure and tone unit boundaries; in Traditional Englishes, it is realized with heightened pitch, volume, and length on the designated prominent syllable. In Indian English, however, Pickering & Wiltshire (2000) found both a dip in pitch on prominent syllables where a pitch peak would be expected and irregular volume changes. These features appeared in the same contexts in which speakers of Traditional Englishes would raise both their pitch and their volume.

We also know that this difference in the phonetic realization of prominence impacts the comprehensibility of Indian English speech for speakers of other varieties. From the perspective of speakers of Traditional Englishes, the low-high pitch pattern on words and lack of reliable volume cues violate listener expectations of a high-low pattern and consistent volume change. Table 7.1 shows some examples from Pandey (1981) and Pickering (1999) of misunderstandings that have occurred in cases where the location of the prominent syllable is misinterpreted due to its phonetic realization in Indian English (IE).

7.2.1.2 Prominence Patterns

Prominence patterns are critical cues used by hearers to follow information sequencing in discourse. Emphatic, or contrastive, stress is found across all varieties of Traditional English and is used for the same functional purposes, including highlighting misunderstood information. However, this is not the case in Indian English.

To demonstrate this, I have recreated an example from an exercise discussed in Gumperz and Roberts (1980). The authors propose that this contrastive pattern is absent in General Indian English and test this using a simple phone

Table 7.1. Misunderstanding of IE Stress by Speakers of Traditional Englishes

Example Word	IE Speaker Says...	Speaker of Traditional English Variety Hears...
defense	DEfense	difference
rendered	renDERED	endured
impedance	IMpedance	impudence

number repetition task in which one digit is repeated incorrectly by a speaker and is then corrected (the digit is marked in bold). Listen to two speakers of Traditional Englishes (TE) complete the dialogue.

    1: TE Speaker A: Ok, what's your phone number?

    2: TE Speaker B: 583-5937

    3: TE Speaker A: 584-5937

    4: TE Speaker B: Oh, no, 58**3**-5937.

SF 7.1

In the first iteration of the digit 3 in Line 2, there is a fall-rise pattern. In the second iteration in Line 4, there is a much higher and more sharply defined falling pattern that is consistent with the placement of emphatic or contrastive stress to mark that single digit as incorrect. Now listen to the same dialogue between a TE speaker and an IE speaker.

    1: TE Speaker: Ok, what's your phone number?

    2: IE Speaker: 583-5937

    3: TE Speaker: 584-5937

    4: IE Speaker: No, 58**3**-5937

SF 7.2

Note that there is no contrastive pitch pattern on the corrected digit. The lack of this specific intonational cue will violate the expectations of speaker-hearers of Traditional Englishes and may lead to frustration or confusion.

7.2.1.3 Substitution of Pitch Register Shifts for Tonal Movement

In Traditional Englishes, the speaker selects a key (high, mid, or low) for each tone unit; and movement between this key choice and the termination choice in the same unit moves in a stepwise pattern between levels. Typically, there are no sudden shifts in pitch register within the tonic segment. Within General Indian English however, there can be frequent and abrupt changes or "leaps" between pitch levels on individual syllables, both within words and across tonic segments. These shifts between levels (or pitch register) in a given speaker's range, often appear in place of tonal movement. This is shown in Figure 7.1.

Figure 7.1.   Pitch Choices by TE and IE Speakers

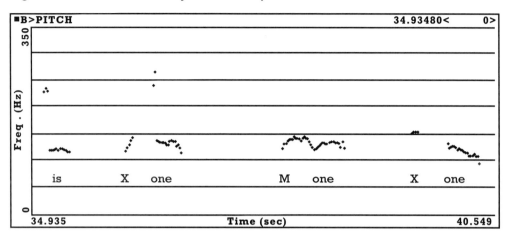

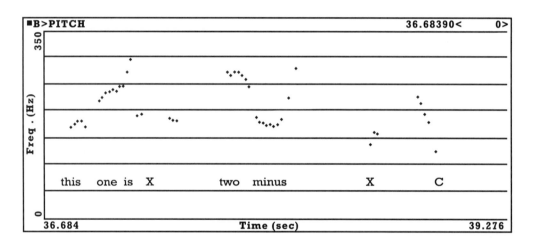

Figure 7.1 shows two pitch traces (pictures of the intonation contours) of very short extracts of lectures given in university physics laboratory classes in North America (Pickering, 1999). In both cases, the teachers are talking through the formulas as they write them on the board. The first pitch track is from a General American English-speaking teacher and comprises three tone units: //⇩IS X ⇨ONE//M ⇨ONE// X ⇩ONE//. There is a rise in pitch level from low to mid as each variable is highlighted and the final unit concludes with a low termination. Pitch level changes are constrained and adjacent.

Contrast this with a similar extract from an Indian English speaker where the three units are "//this ONE IS// X TWO MInus// X C//." They are characterized by leaps in pitch rather than consecutive pitch levels, and it is difficult to assign key or termination choices in the same way as in the General American

English example. The sharp rise on IS contrasts with the level movement in the General American pitch trace, and it is followed by a series of pitch drops and peaks on the remaining syllables that do not form a unified contour.

7.2.1.4 Sub-Contours in Expected Tone Units

The final difference highlighted here is in the typical length of tone units. Within General Indian English, tone units are often considerably shorter and contain more prominent syllables in comparison to the tone units that are typical in Traditional Englishes. This creates a series of sub-contours in which many syllables are made prominent:

> [in Indian English] the sentence is divided into several prosodic pieces corresponding to English phrase rather than clause length units…thus at least intonationally, almost every content word is highlighted. (Gumperz, 1982, p. 121)

In addition, these smaller phrasal units often exhibit a distinct downward pitch movement on their initial stressed syllables, followed by a pitch register shift upward on the final accented syllable of each phrase. Although these are not key choices as we would understand them in Traditional Englishes, we can transcribe the perceived effect using pitch range arrows:

//⇩DO you ⇨WANT// a // ⇩CUP of ⇨TEA//

We can demonstrate this by listening to an Indian English speaker say the same text in Chapter 2. In Figure 7.2 the sub-contours are marked in bold:

Figure 7.2. Division of the Text by an Indian English Speaker

> // **last time//** I was at an airport// I was between planes// and I had to make an important phone call// I looked around// and all the phones were// **busy //** so I waited in line// and waited and waited// **and finally I began to// listen//** to the conversation// **of the guy// who was// talking // on the// phone//** I was waiting to use//

SF 7.3

7.2.1.5 Summary

The intonational features that are specific to GIE can result in incomprehensibility or misinterpretation for speaker-hearers of Traditional Englishes in these areas:

- Differences in the phonetic realization of prominence can result in misinterpretation of lexical stress patterns and difficulty in assessing prominent versus non-prominent syllables.

- Prominence placement does not necessarily indicate important information, and multiple prominences within units make it difficult to assess a speaker's message and distinguish important information from surrounding material.

- Assessment of prominence and tonic syllables is further obfuscated by pitch leaps across the speaker's pitch range.

- Sub-contours create short prosodic pieces that lack a unified intonational contour.

These characteristics constitute a series of miscues that can increase the processing load for a hearer unfamiliar with this variety of English. They violate expectations and require the hearer to make continual adjustments to understand the overall text and their predictions as to what may follow. Listener perception studies suggest that hearers react to the confusion in a number of ways. Difficulties in processing information structure may necessitate hearers replaying parts of the message, which can lead to **listener irritation** (Eisenstein, 1983), which is a response to the loss of redundancy and explicitness in the discourse and increases the chance of error in message transmission.

As an example of this kind of reaction, I have included comments from students in response to General Indian English–speaking teachers reported by Park (2016) that are representative of typical reactions to IE comprehensibility problems:

1. "I had a course taught by a professor from India, I could not fully understand his lectures" (p. 61)

2. *Student*:   Indian professors, their accent is hard to understand....
   Researcher: So with Chinese professors, mostly grammar issues.
   And then with Indian professors, mostly accent. (p. 95)

7.2.2 Southeast Asian Englishes

Examples of new varieties of English in Southeast Asia include Singapore English, Malaysian English, and Filipino English. Similar to the Indian context, access to English education and English usage is not uniform within or across Southeast Asian (see Jenkins, 2009). However, these varieties demonstrate some systematic intonational features that differentiate them from Traditional Englishes and that may impact intercultural communication. Recent research suggests that these differences affect these areas: (1) differences in prominence patterns and tonic syllable placement, (2) unit boundaries, and (3) tone choices.

7.2.2.1 Prominence Patterns and Tonic Syllable Placement

Goh (2001, p. 94) notes that in both Malaysian and Singapore English, prominence patterns will not always derive from information structure as would be anticipated in Traditional Englishes. She suggests that this is due to a preference for sentence-final prominence regardless of the information contained there. Two examples from Singapore English and Malaysian English show how repeated information is highlighted in the final unit as prominent despite the ongoing discourse context in which the information is already understood.

Singapore English:	// it is NOT ONly the as<u>SIGN</u>ments// you have to <u>MARK</u>// but <u>AL</u>so// the <u>NUM</u>ber of assignments// you have to <u>MARK</u>//
Malaysian English:	A: // I didn't <u>KNOW</u>// you LIKED <u>CLASS</u>ical music//
	B: // I've ALways <u>LIKED</u>// CLASSical <u>MU</u>sic//

The pattern is particularly striking when the final stress appears on a typically unstressed pronominal as shown in Singapore English (Goh, 2000, p. 39):

A:	// what is <u>IT</u>//
B:	// DONT <u>ASK</u>// just EAT <u>IT</u> //
X:	// I <u>THOUGHT</u>// you WANTed a black <u>ONE</u>//
Y:	// <u>NO</u>// a <u>BLUE</u>// <u>ONE</u>//

7.2.2.2 Unit Boundaries

Similar to Indian English, these Southeast Asian varieties tend to comprise shorter tone units (or sub-contours) that contain prominent syllables. In many cases, the unit boundaries break up what speakers of Traditional Englishes would expect to be single semantic or syntactic units, as in this example from Singapore English:

//because// I WON't be able//to SEE// the other// TRAFfic LIGHT//

(Goh, 2000, p. 96)

7.2.2.3 Tone Choices

Finally, Goh (2000, p. 97) notes that in both Malaysian and Singapore English, there is a predominance of level and falling tone choices as opposed to the rising and falling tone choices that would typically make up the **prosodic composition** of the discourse in Traditional Englishes. The example from Malaysian English shows Speaker B repeating the word that has already been negotiated (*yesterday*) as not only prominent but also with a falling tone rather than the rising tone that would be expected on old information:

A: // WHERE did you go ↘YESterday//

B: // I WENT to the ↘CINema// ↘YESterday//

In these cases, Platt & Ho (1989) suggest that, in both Malaysian and Singapore varieties of English, the falling tone is used to reiterate an important piece of information. In informal contexts, this emphasis may be signaled by a discourse marker such as *lah*; however, this usage is not appropriate in formal contexts and the intonational cue may be used instead.

7.2.2.4 Summary

Based on this research, speakers of Traditional Englishes may find these areas of difficulty in interpreting the intonation patterns of Southeast Asian Englishes:

- Prominence placement does not necessarily indicate important information, and multiple prominences within units may make it difficult to assess a speaker's message.

♦ Assessment of prominence and nuclear syllables is further obfuscated by shorter units that typically contain sub-contours.

♦ An overuse of falling tones may confuse hearers who expect the tone choice to align with particular discourse-pragmatic meanings, which may not be the case.

7.3. Summary and Pedagogical Implications

It is of course true that there are differences in intonational characteristics across Traditional varieties of English such as between American and Australian English or Canadian and British English. Language users of these varieties likely operate within similar areas of tolerance (Brazil, 1997). Because tone unit structure is equivalent and communicative conventions are largely shared between these Traditional varieties, it is unlikely that speaker intent will be routinely misunderstood. Conversely, the intonation features described in this chapter are likely to fall outside any acceptable range of variation that may be anticipated by speakers of Traditional Englishes, and they will potentially impact the success of interactions between speakers of the different varieties. All speakers use pitch variation of some kind, and these movements will typically be interpreted as intentional choices by the hearer based on their own understanding of the system.

It is important to remember that varieties of New Englishes are successfully used by millions of speakers within their local contexts. However, we are still some way from being able to adequately describe the pragmatic value of the intonational features of many of these varieties (for two recent explorations of African Englishes see Lomotey, 2015, and Ouafeu, 2010).

This is also a good time to remind ourselves that discourse is a cooperative achievement. In other words, interactional success is guided by a principle of co-construction (Duranti, 1986; Jacoby & Ochs, 1995). Both Nelson (1985) and Kang & Rubin (2009) note that a listener who expects to understand a speaker will be more likely to find that speaker comprehensible than one who does not. In this sense, comprehensibility and interactional success are negotiated between speakers, and some will be willing to be more flexible than others. Unfortunately, the research in this area suggests that the higher the stakes are in a given interaction (think for example of an interview room, the classroom, or a doctor's office), the less forgiving speaker-hearers are likely to be (Roberts & Campbell, 2006).

Any discussion of the pedagogical needs of speakers of New Englishes in a Traditional English context is complicated. There is no "one size fits all" solution due to the varietal continuum and cline of bilingualism that is invariably apparent among this group of speakers. In an ESL classroom context, speakers of New Englishes may respond with a positive or neutral reaction to suggested changes in their communication code. However, many are likely to question the appropriateness of this instruction as their own variety is legitimate, and they are not cognizant of the difficulties that speaker-hearers outside their speech community may be encountering.

In other words, these speakers are not "language learners" in the traditional sense of the word, and they often do not respond well to being treated as language learners. While they might recognize that there are differences between the Englishes they hear and speak, they do not automatically perceive this as a deficit (which their North American/British counterparts often do). This point is illustrated by an extract of an interview between a General American English-speaking student interviewer (SI) and an Indian English-speaking graduate student (GS).

> SI: Ok, let's talk about accent. You would have what we term an Indian English accent.
>
> GS: Yeah.
>
> SI: And is this something you were taught in school?
>
> GS: Um, we were not taught to have separate accent, or we were not taught to have an accent at all. It was actually what we saw from the teachers that we got, so. . . .
>
> SI: Right.
>
> GS: So, I would say that Indian English has a characteristic of its own. There is British English, American English and then there should be Indian English. Because it is totally different from everywhere else.[1]

In addition, Indian English speakers would likely approach the acquisition of features of an English variety such as American English very differently from other second language learner groups. Sociolinguistic studies conducted in

---

[1]With thanks to Brenna Seifried for these data.

India (Sahgal, 1991; Sridar, 1997) suggest that speakers prefer to use a General Indian English model. Sahgal found that 47 percent of educated people in Delhi preferred an ordinary Indian English model and only 2 percent of Indian English speakers chose American English as their preferred model. Sridhar (1997) suggests that speakers who come too close to a Traditional English model of speech are considered to be "fundamentally suspect," "phony," "affected," or "snobbish."

When addressing the ESL needs of this group, language analysis is almost always more effective than language instruction. The language adaptations that are being suggested must be clearly motivated and transparent to the speakers, and the best way to do this is to engage the learners in an open discussion of the differences between the varieties. It is also important to emphasize that despite the more familiar patterns that may occur in New English varieties as opposed to second language learner English, there is plenty of room for misinterpretation, and negotiation is crucial.

Finally, ESL instructors are not immune to the kinds of linguistic stereotyping that can arise in the rest of the community. We must remind ourselves that our responses to speakers outside our variety can be critically affected by the kinds of cumulative miscues that have been discussed in this chapter, within the classroom as well as outside it.

7.4. Check Your Learning

1. What do Roberts and Campbell mean when they use the term the linguistic penalty?

2. Describe at least two intonational cues that vary between North American and Indian English.

3. In what ways might Indian English or Southeast Asian students react differently from L2 learner groups in the ESL classroom?

7.5. Activities

1. The effects of perceived accent can range from the positive or benign
   to the very disruptive. Numerous websites list the "top 10 most loved
   English accents." Accents that always appear at the top of these lists
   include the Irish accent and the British English accent. Indian or
   Filipino English accents do not appear. Discuss the ways in which
   perceptions of accent might impact the success of a speaker in a gate-
   keeping encounter such as in a job interview.

2. Expressions of frustration with call-center or outsourced helplines has
   become ubiquitous in the North American and British popular press, as
   illustrated by these two quotes taken from the Times newspaper online
   business news network (business.timesonline.co.uk):

   "I hate Indian call centers that read scripts and have accents that
   you cannot understand."

   "Very often I've had trouble understanding call center staff,
   especially from BT [British Telecom] because of their thick
   Indian accents. All I want is a tech support person that will be
   able to help me. I don't think that makes me a racist."

   What has been your own experience of communicating with call agents
   in this context? Has the information you have read in this chapter
   changed any of your perceptions?

4. In 2005, David Deterding published a study in *TESOL Quarterly* in which he asked Singaporean English speakers to transcribe the speech of speakers of Estuary English—the most commonly heard accent in southeast Britain (see https://www.phon.ucl.ac.uk/home/estuary/estuary.pdf). There were many cases of mistranscription, and Deterding also talks about the "frustration and even anger expressed by many of the listeners" (p. 436). This is one of the first published studies in which a typical comprehensibility study is "turned on its head" and speakers of a New variety of English are asked to judge the intelligibility of a Traditional variety of English. Discuss how studies such as these can help to legitimize alternative varieties of English.

Chapter 8

Variation between Traditional Englishes and English as a Lingua Franca

In an op-ed piece titled "Being a native English speaker is globally useless if you can't speak other versions of English," Spencer Hazel (2016) highlights the dilemma of many business people who find that their use of a Traditional English may "render them incomprehensible" to colleagues and business partners in the international community. Estimates of how many speakers use English as a lingua franca (as a language of communication in a non–English speaking environment) vary, but it is certainly in the millions (Seidlhofer, 2013). In the literature, the "versions" that Hazel alludes to have been variously described as a variety such as International English, a set of sub-varieties such as World Englishes or Global Englishes, and even as a campaign, e.g., the English as an International Language movement (Dauer, 2005, p. 544). The differences between these terms is often not straightforward as researchers in this relatively new field choose definitions that may prioritize the geographical boundaries within which the language is used, the purpose for which it is used, or how it is typically acquired (excellent discussions of these issues can be found in Jenkins, 2009; McKay, 2002; Seidlhofer, 2013).

This chapter explores how intonation is used in the context of English as a Lingua Franca (ELF). For the purposes of this book, ELF is defined as "communication between fairly fluent interlocutors from different L1 backgrounds, for whom English is the most convenient language" (Breiteneder et al., 2006, p. 163). Other definitions are useful in other settings.

The number of speakers of English in non-traditional contexts—that is, those outside of an English-only environment—is rapidly increasing. As Nelson (1995) notes, the native speaker is a rare sight in most international interactions in English, and many speakers "may never have had the dubious good fortune even to have met a native speaker" (p. 276). It is unsurprising then, that an investigation of this context of use suggests that processes by which understanding is achieved in ELF are qualitatively different from those found in interactions between speakers of Traditional Englishes, and that this includes differences in the use of the intonation system. This research is in its early stages, and the data used in this discussion come primarily from two sources (Pickering, 2009; Pickering & Litzenberg, 2011) with additional support when available.

8.1. Characteristics of ELF Interactions

In contrast to the types of interactions discussed in Chapter 7, research in the area of ELF suggests different practices. Specifically, in ELF, speakers employ conversational strategies and accommodation processes that derive from the recognition of a lack of common ground/shared knowledge between speakers, which then prompts them to choose language that is characterized by literal and transparent meaning. This might typically include a reduced use of idiomatic phrases and formulas or an agreement not to assign meaning to linguistic choices unless they appear to be transparent—for example, avoiding figurative or metaphorical language (Cogo & Dewey, 2006; Kecskes, 2006). The next sections show how this principle applies to differences in the use of intonation by dividing the functions of intonation into (1) informational and (2) relational (or interpersonal) functions.

8.2. Use of Intonation for Informational Functions

Chapter 3 discussed how informational functions included using prominence (tonic syllable placement) to mark new information or establish a contrast. This is also true in ELF interactions. Consider this interaction between a Thai L1 speaker (T) and a Korean L1 speaker (K) who are engaged in a "spot the difference" task.

Example 1

    1:    T:// but near that have a big ↘<u>PIC</u>ture//

    2:    K:// before ↗<u>WIN</u>dow//

    3:    T: (looks down at picture, looks back at K and frowns)

    4:    K:// before ↗<u>WIN</u>dow// (small hand gesture)

    5:    T:// not ↘<u>WIN</u>dow//(+) // AH-↘be<u>FORE</u> window// yeah//
        ↘<u>NEXT</u> to window//

    6:    K: (repeats softly) // ↘<u>NEXT</u> to window//

                                             (Pickering, 2009, p. 244)

T is describing a picture that appears in a drawing and is confused when K switches to talking about a window that is also shown in the drawing. In Line 4, K asks again about the window, and in Line 5, T says that he is not talking about the window. He then realizes that K is trying to ask if the picture is placed before (meaning "next") to the window. T indicates he now understands that K means to make the preposition prominent (and not the noun) by repeating the phrase with a nuclear stress on be<u>FORE</u> and then correcting the preposition to <u>NEXT</u>. It is not possible to absolutely affirm that K understands the importance of the misplaced prominence, but he clearly echoes T's prominence pattern in Line 6.

In addition to prominence, the informational function of tone choice also emerges as a feature of ELF interaction. Kecskes (2006, p.10) has noted the importance of "fixed expressions with clear compositional meaning," reflecting the transparency principle previously discussed in this chapter. In our data, such expressions took the form of clarification or comprehension checks (e.g., *yeah*, *right*) that had a fixed lexical and prosodic shape. Examples from two speakers are shown:

Example 2

    Turkish speaker: // it's recTANgular ↗<u>RIGHT</u>//

                          // you have a CARpet ↗<u>YEAH</u>//

    Spanish speaker: // it's the SAME ↗<u>RIGHT</u>//

                          // the sofa is near the TAble ↗<u>RIGHT</u>//

                                           (Pickering, 2009, p. 247)

In interactions between speakers of Traditional Englishes, these types of markers typically appear with a range of tone choices depending on function. However, it appears that in ELF interaction, this function is specialized, and the rising tone choice is essential to its interpretation. Example 3 shows another transparent use of rising tones and falling tones to signal ongoing negotiation routines and to mark their resolution [Spanish L1 speaker (CR); French L1 speaker (C); and Korean L1 speaker (K)]:

Example 3

1:	CR:	// ↗mayBE// // →some <u>CLASS</u>//
2:		// →you can use another [e]stra<u>TE</u>gie-s//
3:		// because [unclear]//
4:		// ↘how do you say <u>THAT</u>// // ↗am- ambi<u>GU</u>-//
5:	C:	// ↗say <u>WHAT</u>//
6:	CR:	// ↗am<u>BI</u>gual//
7:	C:	// ↗am<u>BIG</u>ger//
8:	CR:	// ↗am<u>BIG</u>ger//
9:	C:	// →am<u>BI</u>gu-// [laughs]
10:	K:	// ↗am<u>BIG</u>ger//
11:	C:	// →<u>YEAH</u>// // ↘it's <u>LIKE</u>// // ↘it, it's kind of con<u>FU</u>sion//
12:		// ↘it's con<u>FU</u>sion// [laughter & overlapping speech]

(Pickering & Litzenberg, 2011, p. 81)

SF 8.1

In this excerpt, CR is attempting to say the word *ambiguous* and is assisted by C and K. In Line 4, CR directly asks for help with the word: "How do you say that, *ambigu-*" using a rising tone. The continuing negotiation work is evident in the rising or level tones used by all three participants in Lines 5–10. Finally, in Line 11, C offers a paraphrase with "it's kind of confusion" using a falling tone. The paraphrase is repeated in Line 12, also with a falling tone, and concludes the negotiation routine, despite the lack of a final target form for *ambiguous*. But a similar meaning was achieved or negotiated. Both CR and K accept this falling tone choice as a signal of closure of the routine regarding this particular lexical item and no further negotiation occurs.

Similar findings from Pitzl (2005), who looked at ELF business meetings, suggest that a combination of tonic syllable placement and rising intonation are used as part of an explicit code of communication designed to enhance interactional efficiency and intelligibility.

8.3. Use of Intonation for Interpersonal Functions

The **socially integrative functions** discussed in Chapter 5 and 6 to show agreement, which are crucial in Traditional Englishes, do not systematically appear in ELF interaction. Unlike interaction based in Traditional Englishes in which rising tones are typically used by speakers to avoid the appearance of overt contradiction (Hewings, 1995), ELF speakers do not seem to employ this face-saving device. In Example 4 the Thai speaker (T) directly contradicts the Korean speaker (K) when she misunderstands *table* using a combination of the direct disagreement marker <u>NO</u> and a low, falling tone that might strike speakers of Traditional Englishes as unnecessarily abrupt and rude.

Example 4

      T: //do you have ➚<u>TA</u>ble//

      K: //yeah like ➚<u>TE</u>levision//

      T: //➘<u>NO</u>// ➘<u>TA</u>ble//

(Pickering, 2009, p. 252)

The next example features three ELF participants discussing their preference for morning or evening English classes at an English Language Institute. The Russian (R) and Vietnamese (V) speakers have dominated the conversation, and in an attempt to incorporate the Arabic speaker into the conversation, R directly engages him about his class time preference in Lines 5–6 [Russian L1 speaker (R); Vietnamese L1 speaker (V); Saudi Arabian Arabic L1 speaker (S)]:

Example 5

  🎧 1:   R: //it was the ONE of the reasons why I ➜<u>CHOOSE</u>//

      2:       //this ➘<u>PRO</u>gram because it's//

      3:       //➘<u>MORN</u>ing <u>CLAS</u>ses//

    4:    V: // ↘YEAH//

               [quiet talking, laughing] [3-second pause]

    5:    R: // choose ↘ONE// (++) //which ONE do you ↘LIKE//

    6:        // ↗this ONE// . . . [unclear, laughing]

                               (Pickering & Litzenberg, 2011, p. 83)

SF 8.2

Within Brazil's model, the communicative value of the two falling tones in Line 5 can be understood as something like "I am telling you to choose one," as opposed to the more likely choice in Traditional Englishes of a rising tone that would imply instead "I am asking you to choose one." With the additional use of the imperative, these tone units could sound quite aggressive; however, S does not appear to orient toward the perceived note of impatience or aggression that comes across so strongly to speakers of Traditional Englishes. In an ELF situation, the focus of the interaction may be on informational understanding so nuances of tone are less crucial than they would be if a Traditional English speaker were involved.

    In terms of pitch concord or pitch agreement between participants in conversation, Anderson (1990, p. 107) and others have noted that in native speaker interactions, "concord-breaking will not pass unobserved but be taken as meaningful by speakers" as an indicator of some kind of disagreement. In our ELF data, however, as with tone choices, pitch discord appeared to be not commented on. This example is an interaction between two of the three speakers [Vietnamese L1 speaker (V); Saudi Arabian Arabic L1 speaker (S)]:

Example 6

    1:    V: // how about ⇨YOU//

    2:    S: // uh, about ⇨GRAMmar//

    3:    V: // ⇨YEAH//

    4:    S: // ⇨GRAMmar// I don't th- ⇧LIKE GRAMmar//⇨REALly//

    5:    V: // you ⇧LIKE GRAMmar//

    6:    S: // ⇧ ⇧NO no no no// because . . . /[unclear]

                               (Pickering & Litzenberg, 2011, p. 86)

SF 8.3

The Vietnamese speaker (V) asks the Arabic speaker (S) if he likes grammar, but V mishears the response and in Line 5 checks his understanding by asking "You like grammar." S's response ("NO no no no") is both considerably louder and considerably higher than that of the Vietnamese speaker and sounds unnecessarily forceful. Both the volume (upper box) and pitch (lower box) traces shown in Figure 8.1 confirm this (Pickering, Litzenberg, & Zoll, p. 86).

In the ongoing interaction, none of the speakers seem to orient negatively toward this overt statement of disagreement in a negotiation. This would likely not be the case in an interaction between speakers of Traditional Englishes because to do so could send the wrong message and the goal is agreement.

In sum, ELF users do not use all the aspects of intonation structure and function that appear in Traditional Englishes. Specifically, they do not appear to orient to the use of intonational cues to establish or maintain personal relationships. However, they do use them to signal informational structure. This preferred usage may be a result of ELF speakers' recognition of a lack of a shared linguistic background and a preference for a transparent, explicit code of communication designed to enhance efficiency.

Figure 8.1.   Arabic Speaker Response with Increased Pitch and Volume

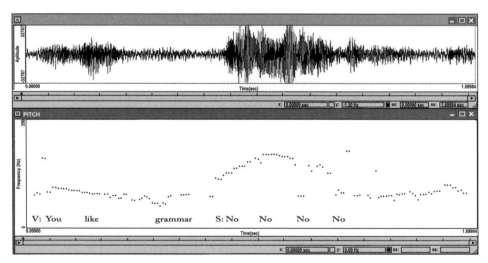

8.4. Intonation Use and Transparency in ELF Interaction

One way to interpret the data from these early analyses is to suggest that the use of rising and falling tones to mark information structure in English is more transparent (i.e., the function is more likely to be recognized by ELF speakers) than the use of intonational features to express interpersonal functions. This would fit with repeated proposals that there is a cross-linguistic similarity in the use of falling intonation to express completeness and rising intonation to express incompleteness that speakers may orient to (Cruttenden, 1997; Mauranen, 2006) and that ELF speakers naturally transfer this into their use of English as a lingua franca (as shown in Example 3). However, the kind of intuition that may account for ELF speakers' use of these cues for informational functions may be much less reliable when applied to the use of intonation for relationship building purposes. This usage may be more opaque and thus not easily oriented to by speakers. Support for this interpretation is shown in Menjo's (2016) study of perception of English intonation patterns by Japanese learners of English. Three groups of learners participated (beginning learners living in Japan; intermediate learners who had been in the U.S. for no more than four years; advanced learners who had been in the U.S. for no less than ten years) and a control group of General American English speakers. The learners listened to a stimulus with a picture on the computer screen and, based on the intonation pattern heard in the stimulus, decided if the speaker liked the item in the picture. The results showed that while the control group was able to successfully assess the feeling of the speaker, the advanced speakers of Japanese proved to be no better than the beginning learners at assessing whether the speaker was expressing like or dislike of the item in the picture. Although this is a perception and not a production study, it may help explain why the ELF speakers did not appear to respond to some of the intonational cues that could have been considered more aggressive by native speakers.

We also need to consider ELF speakers' language learning experiences, particularly in a classroom environment. Mauranen (2006) suggests that instruction may have resulted in learners acquiring certain fixed intonational patterns or "chunks" (like *you know*) in their speech that they then bring to their ELF interactions. This may be the case, for example, with the confirmation checks shown in Example 2. On the other hand, the kinds of relational cues that we have talked about are rarely, if ever, addressed in the classroom or in textbooks (see Chapter 1). Can students manipulate this aspect of English intonation if it is never taught to them?

8.5. Summary and Pedagogical Implications

Interest in the context of English as a Lingua Franca has grown considerably in the TESOL profession over the past decade, and research has shown that linguistic communication strategies can be quite different from those used in other settings. The work reported in this chapter suggests that this is also the case with regard to the use of intonational cues. While participants in ELF interactions use intonation to mark information structure, they do not appear to orient toward relational cues in the same way. Thus it is clear that informational and social convergence are differently achieved in cross-varietal contexts. In terms of intonation features, patterns that have likely developed over time for use in one context may not be easily "unlearned" when speakers find themselves in a different one. This applies, of course, to both ELF speakers and speakers of Traditional Englishes, since both may misunderstand or be misunderstood by the other group. Routines and structures used in ELF interaction, particularly when it comes to interpersonal situations may conflict with the ways in which speakers of Traditional Englishes typically negotiate understanding, which can result in possible miscommunication between speakers in the two groups. This also means that speakers of different varieties will bring their own established strategies to mixed interactions and will find themselves potentially listening for very different things and interpreting the pragmatic message of their interlocutors quite differently.

From a pedagogical perspective, the current shift toward acceptance of multiple varieties of English and multiple contexts of use allows us to take a more nuanced approach to teaching intonation (and indeed, all areas of the English language). For example, we would not necessarily want to promote strategies among non-native speakers that have been shown to increase comprehensibility for native-speaker listeners if the former will be primarily or exclusively engaged in ELF interaction. Conversely, for students who are moving from an ELF context to an English-only environment, we cannot just anticipate certain gaps in their pragmatic competence with regard to intonation structure and function, but must also assume some foundational aspects that we can build from, such as the informational marking previously discussed.

8.6. Check Your Learning

1. Can you define ELF as it is used in this chapter?

2. Identify two "transparent" uses of intonation features in the ELF context. Can you identify two additional intonation features that are less likely to occur in an ELF context?

3. What do Menjo's findings suggest about long-term acquisition of the intonation system by ESL learners?

8.7. Activities

1. A few pronunciation books are now available that focus on the ELF context (for example Walker, 2010). In what ways might you change or adapt your pronunciation focus to accommodate students who are primarily engaged in that environment?

2. Increasingly, researchers are developing their own large ELF corpora in order to study the emerging features of this variety. Two major corpora are based in Europe: the Vienna-Oxford International Corpus of English (VOICE) at https://www.uni/ac/at/voice// and the Corpus of English as an Academic Lingua Franca at the University of Helsinki (ELFA) at http://www.helsinki.fi/varieng/CoRD/corpora/ELFA.

   One is in Asia: the Asian Corpus of English at the Hong Kong Institute of Education (ACE) at http://www.corpus.ied.edu.hk/ace/About.html.

   Choose one of these corpora and go to the website. How easy is it to navigate? What information can you find out about phonological features?

3. The Association of Southeast Asian Nations (ASEAN) is made up of ten countries (Brunei, Cambodia, Indonesia, Laos, Malaysia, Myanmar, the Philippines, Singapore, Thailand, and Vietnam). Deterding & Kirkpatrick (2006) investigated the pronunciation features of interactions within ASEAN. Examples from their data are presented. Decide in what ways these prosodic choices are different from those that would appear in Traditional Englishes. (<u>Hint</u>: This is also called **heavy end stress**.)

   1. er we do not er teach grammar the incidental <u>WAY</u>

   2. because there are a lot of students who are weak in English and they go to such schools just to learn <u>ENGLISH</u>

   3. I love teaching and I enjoy <u>TEACHING</u>

   4. It was meant for only a h- a holiday a three-day <u>HOLIDAY</u>

   5. Erm English is very new and very few people speak <u>ENGLISH</u>

Chapter 9

Teaching Discourse Intonation

A pilot study tested ESL students' awareness of the functions of intonation, including the meaning of marked intonation patterns such as

//the TEACHer didn't grade your papers// (i.e., someone else did)

The study noted that most of the students consistently missed the implication carried by the intonation pattern and rejected its importance; one student even "explicitly questioned" the idea that the meaning could be carried by the intonation, stating that "if this [intonation] is really important, someone would have told us by now" (Reed & Michaud, 2015, p. 461).

This anecdote very eloquently points to the gap that continues to exist between research and classroom practice in the area of intonation. Indeed, it is not only students, but also teachers, who express doubts as to the benefits of spending significant amounts of classroom time on intonation. Thus, this chapter focuses on a frequently asked question: Is the intonation system in English both teachable and learnable? Considering how often the terms *unteachable* and *unlearnable* have been associated with the idea of teaching intonation structure in English, it may come as a surprise to readers to hear that there is, in fact, plenty of evidence to counteract these claims in several different research paradigms. Research in each paradigm is briefly addressed next.

9.1. Experimental Evidence

Three recent syntheses of empirical investigations in general pronunciation instruction (Lee, Jang, & Plonsky, 2015; Saito, 2012; Thomson & Derwing, 2015) confirm that, as a general rule, pronunciation instruction is effective in both classroom and laboratory settings.

Lee, Jang, & Plonsky (2015) reviewed 86 studies and found that positive effects were consistently found for all aspects of pronunciation including **suprasegmentals** and that these effects were "relatively strong and stable" (p. 361). They concluded that, "compared with meta-analytic findings in other areas of instructed SLA, these results show that instruction on pronunciation can be just as (or more) effective as vocabulary, grammar, and pragmatics (p. 357)."

A companion narrative review (Thomson & Derwing, 2015) of 75 studies concurred and reported that "based on the studies surveyed, pronunciation instruction is quite effective and usually leads to significant improvement" (p. 338).

The third, much smaller meta-analysis (15 studies) focused exclusively on those that had a pre- and post-test design methodology in pronunciation (Saito, 2012). Three of the 15 focused on suprasegmentals including speaking rate, rhythm, and prominence (Derwing, Munro, and Wiebe, 1997, 1998; Kennedy & Trofimovich, 2010). In all cases, participants demonstrated improvement at a controlled level (i.e., using reading tasks). Furthermore, Derwing, Munro, & Wiebe's (1998) study included improvement in extemporaneous speaking, which would be more consistent with the focus on spontaneous discourse presented in this book.

In another study, Ramírez Verdugo (2006) conducted a pre- and post-study in which an experimental group of Spanish learners of English were given 10 weeks of training in English intonation including explicit information on the forms and functions of intonation and practice using audio and visual displays of pitch contours. The control group received no specific training. At the end of the study, speakers in the experimental group displayed a significant improvement in their production of tone unit structure, prominent syllables, and tone choice. They were also judged as significantly more intelligible by native speaker raters who made comments such as, "The intonation was very good and helped convey a particular message" (p. 150).

Saito & Saito (2016) provided an experimental group of 10 beginner-level Japanese EFL learners with form-focused instruction in word stress and intonation over a six-week period. When performing read-aloud tasks, the group showed significant gains in all the areas tested, which suggests that instruction can be beneficial even for lower-proficiency learners.

Another study also found that explicit instruction improved performance on suprasegmentals. Using three intact ESL classes, Gordon & Darcy (2016) gave one class explicit instruction in suprasegmentals, while the second class focused on explicit instruction in vowels and the third had non-explicit instruction over a three-week period. Native speaker raters noted significant comprehensibility gains in speakers in the suprasegmental group. Thus, the authors observe that "it is possible to effectively instruct L2 learners in pronunciation in real classroom contexts and in a short time frame" (p. 84). There are clearly lacunae in the experimental research—most notably, a lack of longitudinal follow-up studies and a primary focus on read-aloud speech as opposed to naturally occurring discourse. However, these studies provide consistent and robust findings in favor of intonation instruction.

9.2. Studies of Teacher Cognition

A second lens through which to view the effectiveness of pronunciation teaching is by way of the perceptions of pre-service and in-service teachers. Some research has shown that new teachers may be reluctant to teach pronunciation due to an actual or perceived lack of training in ESL/EFL settings (Baker, 2011; Macdonald, 2002) even though teachers also seem to believe that instruction in suprasegmentals will help their students (Foote, Holtby & Derwing, 2012).

In one course in pronunciation pedagogy in Australia (Burri, 2015), pre-service teachers (both native and non-native speakers) reported an increased sense of confidence in their ability to teach suprasegmentals. The native English speakers stated that they now understood that they could approach this area of instruction in a principled way. One participant said: "All these years I've been teaching various things and to actually get a term, as simple as the word 'prominence,' which I probably should have known, but I had never come across before . . . so for me it's like putting together a jigsaw puzzle (p. 73)." The non-native speakers reported that this course was in some ways their introduction to parts of the sound system of English: "Before I studied this subject, my interest was on segmentals. I wanted to learn segmentals and how to teach native-like sounds, [but] my focus shifted into suprasegmentals and sentence stress and prominence and rhythm and intonation. Those sounds I think should be focused on more (p. 73–74)."

Thus research suggests that pre-service teachers benefit from opportunities to gain training and familiarity in pronunciation pedagogy, which includes suprasegmentals. Interestingly, many master's programs do not require such a course (Murphy, 2014).

9.3. Raising Students' Consciousness

The effect of suprasegmental instruction can be considered through studies that have focused on raising students' awareness of these concepts. Mitrofanova (2012) conducted an experiment with intermediate Russian learners of English in which two groups of participants studied English intonation for 10 weeks. The first group of participants focused on intonational forms and functions with a discourse focus, rather than on imitative production activities. Students identified pitch sequence units and discussed their communicative form and function. They also traced the importance of individual tone choices and prominences in communicating the overall message of the discourse. The second group was taught intonation in a more "traditional" way, and activities focused largely on single tone groups. Following instruction, the production of both groups was assessed by two experienced English teachers. Although no inferential statistics are reported, the differences between the mean scores of the two groups when evaluated for information structuring and intonation performance were marked in favor of the first group (mean scores were 43 percent higher than those for the second group). The assessors also observed that intonation contrasts between given and new information, between different types of nuclear syllables and increased pitch range were stronger in students from the first group.

Similarly, Kennedy & Trofimovich (2010) investigated student awareness of suprasegmentals (thought groups, word stress, rhythm, prominence, and intonation) in a 13-week course for intermediate learners. They report that dialogue journals written by the students showed an increased awareness of suprasegmental features.

9.4. Summary and Pedagogical Implications

Taken as a whole, the research indicates that intonation is both teachable and learnable at all proficiency levels and in different classroom contexts using a variety of techniques. The effectiveness of instruction focused on individual systems (tone choice, prominence, pitch range, and tone unit structure) suggests that a model such as the one presented here will successfully address the most typical issues that arise with the intonation system of English. A possible model focusing specifically on the ITA context is shown in Gorsuch et al. (2013).

Accepting that discourse intonation can and should be taught in the classroom if teachers are given the right preparation and students value the instruction, how would this be implemented? Before considering specific suggestions, a few overall issues must be examined.

1. **Proficiency level**. There is now agreement that pronunciation instruction, including suprasegmentals, should be incorporated into language teaching from the very beginning (Chela-Flores, 2008; Zielinshi & Yates, 2014). Derwing & Munro (2005) have suggested that such instruction may result in faster improvement at lower levels. It is also important that explicit attention and feedback be given to learners in this area at all proficiency levels (Yates & Zielinski, 2009).

2. **Teaching context** and **specific learner goals**. In terms of ITAs (see Chapter 6), the ability to both produce and perceive discourse intonation can be critical to their success in the classroom. Other similarly high-stakes contexts include workplace environments in which transnationals may suffer from the linguistic penalty (see Chapter 7). It is important to remember, however, that not all learners are preparing for these contexts of use. Teachers of second language speakers who are focused on settings in which New or Emerging Englishes are the norm may want to take a different approach that takes into consideration other communicative needs/goals (see Chapter 8).

3. **Correction and forgiveness**. A common question from learners is something like: "do I have to get all these choices right, all of the time?" The answer is almost certainly no. It is important to remember that the effect of intonational miscues described here is cumulative. That is, any negative perceptions that might result for hearers will occur over time not as the result of an individual intonation choice. It is not uncommon for any speaker to realize only when uttering a tone unit that the choice was perceived differently by the hearer than intended.

9.4.1 Teaching Suggestions

In the teaching of pronunciation—especially intonation—here are some general guidelines to help students improve.

- ◆ Tone Unit Structure and Prominence
  1. Reading aloud short passages from authentic discourse (see, for example, Chapter 2) can be used to promote thought group fluency and prominence patterns for low-proficiency learners. As the morphological and syntactic content is specified, students can focus on their suprasegmental production.

2. Giving presentations of any length improves thought group
    fluency for intermediate and advanced learners by building
    sensitivity to tone unit boundaries and pause structure.
    Presentations can also be used to develop understanding of topic-
    sensitive prominence choices (e.g., when contrasting two pieces
    of information). Scripted or read-aloud speech is not advocated
    at these proficiency levels because it can encourage memorization
    rather than real-time production and this will significantly
    alter intonation choices. However, preparation and practice
    of presentations based on previously constructed outlines is
    recommended to reduce the hesitations and stumbles that result
    from completely unplanned oral production (Pickering, 2004).

◆ Tone Choice

1. Information gap tasks can be designed for any proficiency
    level to focus both on tone choice for informational purposes
    and to discuss the role of tone choice in establishing friendly
    cooperation. In this sense, collaborative tasks such as jigsaw
    information gap tasks can show students how to establish
    stronger social relations through their speech (Donato, 2004).

2. Roleplay is another activity that can be used to focus on tone
    choice; particularly if the roles incorporate asymmetrical
    interaction, i.e., a teacher and a student or a manager and an
    employee. This can be used to highlight the more nuanced
    pragmatic values of dominant versus non-dominant tone choices
    as well as the use of solidarity markers such as *you know* or *ok*.

◆ Key and Termination Choice

1. The use of recorded conversational interactions is a way that
    intermediate and advanced students can examine the role of key
    and termination in turn-taking and pitch matching.

2. Narratives (e.g., picture stories) can be used to highlight the role
    of pitch paragraphing as speakers transition from one part of the
    story to the next. Samples of picture stories are widely available
    on the internet. One text that I have used is *Sequences: Picture
    Stories for ESL* (Chabot, 2006).

Two types of activities that could be used at the intermediate and advanced levels to address discourse intonation as a whole through the use of language analysis and practice are included in Appendixes A and B. The first is a description (with research behind it) of the Mirroring Project developed by Meyers (2014) in which students choose a model speaker, preferably a "high-achieving, accented, intelligible, comprehensible ESL speaker" and choose a short video clip or model or "mirror." By mirroring the speaker's prosodic and paralinguistic behavior, students get a sense of what English prosodic structure *feels* like (see also Discussion Activity 3.9 #4 on p. 62 in Meyers, 2014).

The second activity (with all materials provided) is ready to use. In *An Election: Running for Class President,* created by DeGaytan & DeGaytan (2012), students evaluate a speech given by a character in a movie. They then work through a series of tasks in which they create their own speeches while focusing on prosody and delivery.

9.5. Check Your Learning

1. What does the research evidence suggest regarding the teachability and learnability of intonation in English?

2. Why is context of use important to consider when choosing how to teach discourse intonation?

3. Why is it important to consider mode of discourse when teaching the systems that comprise discourse intonation?

9.6. Activities

1. Fill in the gaps in the chart with appropriate activities after considering student proficiency level and the system being focused on. Note that priorities for advanced learners will depend on their specific needs. Choose one learner population at an advanced level and set your first two priorities.

Proficiency Level	Chunking*	Prominence	Tone	Key
Beginning Priority: Understanding tone unit structure				
Intermediate Priorities: (1) Establishing friendly co-operation (2) Elucidating information structure				
Advanced Priorities: (1) (2)				

* Chunking is the creation of tone units and effective pause structure.

2. The Appendixes include activities that address the discourse intonation system as a whole. In both cases, students begin with language analysis using the transcripts. Why is language analysis an effective way to address the production and perception of discourse intonation?

Chapter 10

Putting It All Together

The central aims of this book have been to describe an approach to intonation in English discourse that is both systematic and comprehensive and to demonstrate its relevance for ESL/EFL contexts. The final chapter reviews the components of the model and revisits the central positions related to intonation and language teaching. We close with a brief discussion of some of the questions regarding discourse intonation that are of further interest.

10.1. The Model

Some of the essential understandings we have reached with regard to intonation and language teaching are:

- **The intonation system is probabilistic yet systematic.** We can predict what is likely (or conversely, unlikely) to happen based on previous linguistic experience, but we cannot predict in absolute terms what speakers will say and how listeners will interpret it. Because the system is speaker-controlled and hearer-sensitive, we can situate probable usage within the conventions of a given speech community and a particular speech event (e.g., a North American university classroom), and this can allow us to examine the patterns that typically occur in this specific environment. In order to reveal any patterns, however, the framework must be both comprehensive and flexible enough to accommodate new possible structures. As an example, recall the Pierrehumbert & Hirschberg (1990) AM model of intonation in discourse (see Chapter 2). Although the model describes the relationships that can be created between individual intonation units by focusing on right edge boundary tones, there is no regularization of a left edge boundary tone (or **key** in Brazil's terms). The focus on this left edge boundary in the model has allowed for continued and detailed investigation of the role of pitch concord between speakers and increased awareness of speech paragraphs marked by initial and final pitch choices. This kind of flexibility is important in order to facilitate insight into possible speech events. It also allows us to expand our teaching presentations to include text-level, as opposed to sentence-level, treatments of intonation. Sample exercises with one structure can be found in Levis & Pickering (2004) and Gorsuch et al. (2013).

◆ **The intonation system works within a discourse context.** As the discourse-pragmatic nature of intonational meaning would presuppose, intonation choices interact with each other, the specific context of the interaction, and the perceived relationship between speaker and hearer. When these choices are isolated from one another by focusing on individual utterances without context, it becomes much more complicated to piece the system together. It also becomes more difficult to see the ways in which the intonation system works in conjunction with other linguistic systems (lexical, syntactic, nonverbal) to create clusters of discourse cues that increase the overall coherence of the communicative message for hearers. An integrated analysis of discourse structure demonstrates that it is an accumulation of these signals within the situational context of the interaction that helps hearers to identify manageable chunks of related information and maximal breaks between them.

Pedagogical activities that promote consideration of multiple discourse cues, such as micro-teaching presentations, can be recorded and reviewed for evidence of effective boundary marking across linguistic and non-verbal systems.

◆ **The intonation system can and should be taught.** Can and should the system be taught in the language classroom? Or, can we assume some kind of acquisition of the system based on cross-linguistic similarities in for example, the function of rising and falling intonation? It is important to be cautious here because although we can speculate regarding the possible universal uses of pitch function, there is increasing evidence that some important functions of intonation in English (i.e., relational functions) are not transparent enough to be simply "picked up" by speakers through simple immersion in the language without additional help.

◆ **The structure and function of the intonation system will vary across varieties of English.** At a recent seminar I conducted, a participant expressed disbelief as to the critical role of intonation cues in the cross-cultural interaction described in Chapters 7 and 8. His claim was that we then must be mis-understanding each other much of the time. Although it depends on what precisely is meant by misunderstanding, it is highly probable, even likely, that there may be lack of clarity regarding speaker intent on a fairly frequent basis—or, at the very least, that we may be made uncomfortable to some degree by a speaker's choice of prosodic expression. Effective communication begins with the assumption of co-operative interaction, and speaker-hearers may routinely attempt to ignore the parts that seem questionable, as in a seemingly over-emphatic stress choice or a sudden unexpected and jarring high pitch choice. However, the effects are cumulative, and in high-stakes environments particularly, we may be less willing to overlook them. Recent research suggests that this understanding is even accommodated in ELF interactions in Emerging Englishes with speaker-hearers' preference for transparent and explicit uses of the intonation system (e.g., clear informational signals) as opposed to less well understood, more opaque relational cues. As suggested in Chapter 8, these observations have direct application to our classroom practice as we tailor our presentations to the specific needs of our students. For example, documentation of past experience with English interaction and detailed needs analyses can be used to establish priorities in presentation and practice of the intonation system.

However thoroughly this model has treated the intonation system in English, there remain some open questions. The model was designed to describe the structure and function of intonation in Traditional varieties of English. As we continue to apply it to New and Emerging varieties, it is important to question how well it may describe specific phenomena in these grammatical systems. For example, if we built a model starting from New or Emerging varieties, would it look similar to this one or would there be significant differences?

From a pedagogical perspective for ESL speakers, a question remains as to where the boundary lies between "unremarkable" communication and problematic communication, particularly between speakers of different varieties. To put it differently, when is good "good enough"? At what point is the production of English language learner intonation within the range of tolerance for a native speaker of a Traditional variety in terms of the expression of informational and relational intent? Finally, a comprehensive study testing the effectiveness of the model shown here needs to be implemented in the classroom in order to empirically confirm the pedagogical validity of the theory.

APPENDIX A

Mirroring Project Update: Intelligible Accented Speakers as Pronunciation Models

Colleen M. Meyers, M.A., educational specialist, International Teaching Assistant Program, Center for Teaching & Learning, University of Minnesota,

Have you ever considered using intelligible accented speakers, such as Javier Bardem, as pronunciation models for improving your students' English pronunciation? Native-speaker models often prove challenging while non-native speaking models CAN be a better choice! Learn how to guide your students in choosing an appropriate model, and take them through the process of "mirroring" that model effectively.

Recent research has shown that "high-achieving, accented, intelligible, comprehensible ESL speakers may prove to be excellent pronunciation models for L2 learners." (Murphy, 2011). The project described is an application of this research. An L2 speaker of English (L1 Chinese) used a video on Ted.com by Yang Lan, a.k.a. the "Oprah of China" and a highly intelligible speaker of English," to "mirror" (serve as her model) in order to acquire a more "listener friendly" English pronunciation (Kjellin, 2006) for teaching accounting in a U.S. university setting.

During this presentation, participants were taken through a step-by step process on how to guide their students in: (1) identifying major aspects of pronunciation interfering with comprehensibility; (2) choosing and analyzing an appropriate NNS model to mirror; and (3) assessing improvement in performance of the project from their "cold" (initial) version to their "final" version.

During the first step of the process, participants viewed a micro-teaching presentation by "Mary," an international Teaching Assistant (TA) from China. Participants analyzed her strengths and weaknesses in terms of language and identified two major areas of weakness: (1) lack of focal stress and pitch patterns to highlight important information and (2) use of static non-verbal communication—e.g., rare use of space, gestures, or facial expressions. Mary's segmentals, or pronunciation of individual sounds, on the other hand, were quite good.

In part two, participants were told that Mary had chosen part of a Ted.com talk by Yang Lan as her pronunciation model. They were asked to analyze the talk as to why Mary may have selected this speaker. This crucial step is important for two reasons: (1) students need to search for a role model with whom they feel comfortable and (2) they need to find a comprehensible and intelligible L2 model who is well-suited to the pronunciation feature(s) which they specifically need—e.g., rhythm, intonation, etc. Participants focused on several areas in which Yang Lan was highly proficient, as well as being an excellent model: Even though Ms. Lan still has a bit of an accent, her clear thought groups and stress and intonation patterns make her message easy to follow. In addition, her non-verbal communication (smile, gestures, use of space) conveys confidence and rapport, which are aspects Mary was sorely lacking in as she prepared to teach accounting to undergraduate students at a U.S. university.

There are a few other tips to help students select a suitable role model. First, encourage them to find a segment that is very short, e.g., around 7–10 consecutive sentences. Students often want to mirror larger segments but, since the goal is imitation, this shorter length not only is doable but also long enough to give the segment meaning. Furthermore, a segment from a film, speech, or other YouTube video with strong emotion and/or an important message works well. Yang Lan, for instance is humorous, charismatic, and persuasive—all in the span of one minute and 18 seconds! Finally, the chosen video should be similar to the speaking environment that the student is preparing for in terms of audience and level of formality. Yang Lan was an excellent choice for Mary because she was doing public speaking in a somewhat interactive style, similar to what Mary would be doing when teaching accounting to U.S. undergrads.

In the third part, TESOL participants walked through the Mirroring Project from beginning to end, viewing Mary's "cold version," as well as her final version of the project to assess her improvement. Most agreed that she had done an excellent job on the project, clearly mirroring the areas which she had identified as being weakest early on in the project. Time was set aside for conference participants to discuss ways in which they could use and/or adapt the project to their own teaching environments.

The materials used during the session, including a list of possible NNS models from a variety of L1 backgrounds, and the videos viewed are available online at the following websites:
https://www.dropbox.com/s/uqo08qzn5fcbb3d/MP%20Instructions%20Final%20Version.docx
https://www.dropbox.com/s/fe2frn3mf68tw9n/Possible%20NNS%20Models%20Final%20Version.docx

Mary Micro-Teaching #1:
http://mediamill.cla.umn.edu/mediamill/embed.php?subclip_id=3447&live=true&chrome=true

Mary: "cold" version of Mirroring Project:
http://mediamill.cla.umn.edu/mediamill/display/156112

Mary: "final" version of Mirroring Project:
http://mediamill.cla.umn.edu/mediamill/display/157042

REFERENCES

Brodskey, J. (2006). And thus the upward spiral soars: Notes on Dr. Olle Kjellin's pronunciation teaching method. Retrieved at http://www.k-way.home.sonic.net/

Kjellin, O. (2012). Welcome to Olle Kjellin, the Swedish speech doctor's web page! Retrieved at http://www.olle-kjellin.com/SpeechDoctor/

Lan, Y. (2011). Yang Lan: The generation that's remaking China. Ted Talks. Retrieved at http://www.ted.com/talks/lang/en/yang_lan.html

Murphy, J. (2011). Models for pronunciation instruction: High-achieving, accented, intelligible comprehensible ESL speakers. TESOL Conference, SPLIS Academic Session, New Orleans, Louisiana.

APPENDIX B

An Election: Running for Class President

Catherine DeGaytan & Mark DeGayton, ESL Specialists, Mesa, AZ

Summary

A clip from the movie *Election*, in which two high school students are making speeches in an election for Student Body President, is the springboard for an engaging activity for high-intermediate and advanced students to practice the suprasegmentals (word stress, rhythm, and intonation) and incorporate appropriate delivery skills for an effective speech. An election for Class President is held with each student making the identical speech of the weaker candidate in the movie clip. By making a speech with the same words, students realize that how something is said is just as important as what is said. In addition to improving pronunciation and delivery skills, the activity boosts self-confidence, builds community within the classroom, and helps students make better presentations in the future.

Materials:

> *Election* (directed by Alexander Payne, 1999)
> Transcript of Paul's Speech
> Ballots (slips of paper)
> Evaluation Form
> Self-Evaluation/Reflection Form

Step 1: The Movie Clip

- ◆ Set the scene, give necessary background information, and pre-teach vocabulary before showing the movie clip of the two candidates (Paul and Tammy) making their speeches in the election for Student Body President at Carver High School.
- ◆ View the *Election* clip [Scene 7 "Pathetic Promises"; Time 38:35-42:13] and decide who makes a better speech and why.
- ◆ Ask pairs to discuss their choice for President and reasons for that choice.
- ◆ Wrap up as a class by asking who made the better speech and by eliciting important pronunciation features and delivery skills.

Pronunciation	Delivery Skills
Thought Groups and Pauses	Voice (volume and speaking rate)
Intonation	Eye Contact
Word Stress	Facial Expression
Rhythm	Gestures
Focus Words (emphasized key words)	Posture and Movement
Linking	Vitality

Step 2: Preparation for the Election

- ◆ Explain the activity—giving Paul's election speech with improved delivery skills and appropriate word stress, rhythm, and intonation.
- ◆ View two recorded speeches of former ESL students performing the activity.
- ◆ Ask students to practice the speech in small groups of three or four, each time focusing on a different pronunciation feature with the final practice focusing on delivery skills. Vary the groups each time they practice so that students can work with as many classmates as possible.
- ◆ Ask students to mark the transcript (Form A) of Paul's speech with pause marks for homework before the first in-class group practice.

    Thought Groups, Pauses, and Intonation
    - ◊ Comparing Pause Marks (Then share the teacher's marked transcript.)
    - ◊ Reviewing Intonation
    - ◊ Group Feedback (compliments and suggestions for improvement)

    Word Stress and Rhythm
    - ◊ Underlining Stressed Words
    - ◊ Reviewing Word Stress
    - ◊ Round Robin Reading (with the teacher's marked transcript)
    - ◊ Group Feedback

    Focus Words (emphasized key words)
    - ◊ Highlighting/Circling Focus Words
    - ◊ Shadowing
    - ◊ Group Feedback

    Linking
    - ◊ Marking Linked Words
    - ◊ Group Feedback

    Delivery Skills
    - ◊ Group Feedback
- ◆ Hold individual tutorials (if students desire).
- ◆ Encourage students to practice outside class by speaking in front of a mirror or in front of friends, audiorecording or videorecording themselves, and watching speeches on TV or on the internet.
- ◆ Determine the order of the student "candidates" for Election Day.

Step 3: Election Day Activities

- ◆ Write the names of the student "candidates" on the board in the order in which they will make their speeches. Give every student a ballot (a slip of paper) to vote anonymously for the person who made the best speech and the reason/s why that candidate deserves to win the election.
- ◆ View the video of Paul's speech a second time.
- ◆ Record the students' speeches.
- ◆ Collect the ballots. Ask a student to act as an assistant to tally the votes as the ballots are read aloud.
- ◆ Congratulate the candidate with the most votes—the Class President. A Vice President could also be elected. Praise all of the candidates for being better than Paul, a native speaker of English.

Step 4: Assessment

- ◆ Upload recorded speeches to the online course management system (or other repository) for students to complete one or more of the following: a self-evaluation (Form B), peer evaluation, and reflection. The ballots serve as assessment for those candidates who received votes.
- ◆ Evaluate (Form C) each student's speech in writing.

FORM A

Help Paul improve his speech by marking the important pronunciation features below.

/ = short pause after a thought group
/ / = long pause after a thought group at the end of a sentence

Paul Metzler's Speech

As many of you know I broke my leg pretty bad this year and

the experience has made me re-evaluate what I want to do

with my life and that is help people when you think about it a

school is more than a school it's our second home where we

spend all our time and grow as individuals and a community but

is our school everything it could be I want our school to reach

its true potential that's why I'm running for president I know what

it is to fight hard and win like when we almost went to State

last fall and I threw the fourth quarter pass against Westside for

the touchdown that won the game by three points I won't let

you down like I didn't then and I promise we can all score a

winning touchdown together vote Paul Metzler for president thank you

FORM B

SELF-EVALUATION/REFLECTION: PAUL'S SPEECH

Name_____

<u>Directions</u>: Watch your recorded speech to evaluate your performance.

1. Consider your pronunciation (volume, speaking rate, thought groups and pauses, intonation, word stress, rhythm, focus words, linking, final –s, and problem sounds). What are your strengths? What areas do you think you need to work on?

2. Consider your delivery skills (eye contact, facial expression, gestures, posture and movement, and vitality). What do you think is your greatest strength? Which skills do you need to work on, and how will you try to improve them for your next speech?

3. Did you like making Paul's speech? Did you enjoy the assignment? Why or why not?

FORM C

EVALUATION: PAUL'S SPEECH

Name_____

| = very good | = satisfactory | = needs improvement |

DELIVERY SKILLS

_____ Eye Contact

_____ Facial Expression

_____ Gestures

_____ Posture and Movement

_____ Vitality

PRONUNCIATION

_____ Volume

_____ Speaking Rate (not too fast or too slow)

_____ Thought Groups and Pauses

_____ Intonation

_____ Word Stress

_____ Rhythm

_____ Focus Words

_____ Linking

_____ Final -s

_____ Problem Sounds

Glossary

asides: Parenthetical remarks or brief digressions away from the topic that typically have a lower pitch than the surrounding information.

asymmetrical interaction: An interaction in which there are different levels of power (asymmetry) between the participants, such as in doctor-patient interaction.

attitudinal meaning: Traditional definitions of the affective function of intonation to indicate attitudes and emotions; also called *affective meaning*.

autosegmental-metrical approach: An approach to intonation structure derived from autosegmental phonology (a non-linear approach to the description of phonological approaches) and exemplified in the work of Janet Pierrehumbert. ToBI (tone and break indices) is the associated transcription system.

binding discourse: Discourse in which what is said commits the speakers to something, such as students taking instructions from a teacher in the classroom.

calling contour: An idiomatic combination of a high to low pitch that is associated with the speech act of calling.

cline of proficiency: A description of the different linguistic facility shown by speakers within varieties of New English; also known as a *cline of bilingualism* or a *varietal continuum*.

common ground: The part of linguistic and general non-linguistic context that is assumed to be known by all participants in a given interaction; also called *shared knowledge*.

concord-breaking: A mismatch of prosodic cues such as pitch range or rhythm between participants, also called **prosodic non-matching** (see pitch concord).

confirmation marker: Discourse markers such as *right* or *ok* that project understanding or agreement.

contour analysis: An approach to intonation analysis within the North American tradition that identifies configurations of pitch.

conventions: Linguistic behaviors that have become codified with a speech community and are recognized as having a specific pragmatic meaning; also called *conventionalized norms*.

creaky voice: Low vocal register in which phonation is produced in pulses through a loose glottal closure; also called *vocal fry*.

digital speech processing: The study of the speech signal using a digital representation.

direct orientation: Spoken discourse comprised of intonation choices made by the speaker to benefit the hearer's comprehension, such as toward creating a state of convergence (see oblique orientation).

discourse intonation: Discourse-pragmatic approach to intonation structure and function in English developed by David Brazil (1985/1997).

dominant tones: Rise and rise-fall tone choices that are the prerogative of the controller of the discourse or the participant who claims control.

echo question: A question that partially or completely repeats the syntax of a previous utterance using a rising intonation.

emerging Englishes: English varieties in territories where English is taught as a foreign language.

English as a Lingua Franca (ELF): The use of English as the language of communication between speakers from other languages.

extra-linguistic features: Communicative features that are not part of the linguistic system including kinesics, proxemics, and other forms of non-linguistic information

formulaic language: Linguistic expressions (form + meaning combinations) that are codified but not necessarily fixed and that are associated with specific pragmatic functions, such as clarification or confirmation checks with fixed lexical and prosodic shapes such as *yeah* or *right*; also called *prepackaged chunks*.

functionalist tradition: Linguistic approaches that are concerned primarily with language function, such as M.A.K. Halliday's work.

generative tradition: Linguistic approaches that focus on formalisms, such as "a Chomskyian approach."

heavy end stress: Choice of prominence in some New and Emerging varieties of English on the last word in the tone unit regardless of its informational value.

impression management: The process by which people attempt to influence the perceptions of themselves by other people using linguistic and non-linguistic means.

indexical meaning: A function of intonation that marks speakers' affiliation with regional or socio-cultural groups.

institutional talk: Interactions between speakers within an institutional frame, such as office talk or classroom talk.

intercultural communication: Communication that occurs between people from different cultural/ethnic groups. Also called cross-cultural communication.

intermediate prominences: Prominent syllables that may appear between the onset and final prominences that form the tonic segment.

key: Linguistically significant use of pitch level on the onset prominent syllable divided into a three term system: High key = particularizing function; Mid key = additive function; Low key = reformulating function.

lexical stress: Word-level syllable stress.

linguistic cues: Patterns found in the linguistic systems of any given language variety that are used by participants to understand the communicative message based on their shared linguistic and socio-cultural background; also known as *linguistic devices*.

linguistic penalty: The use of culturally specific communication styles that may affect transnationals' ability to talk in institutionally credible ways in high- stakes situations such as job interviews.

listener irritation: A dual response to non-native discourse by native speakers comprising a negative cognitive reaction to reduced comprehensibility and a negative emotional reaction due to annoyance and distraction.

mishearings: Also known as "slips of the ear," these occur when the hearer mishears and unaware of their misunderstanding.

neutral tone: Level tone choice.

New Englishes: English varieties arising from the second diaspora such as Indian or African Englishes.

oblique orientation: Spoken discourse comprised of intonation choices made by the speaker that are oriented toward the language itself rather than the hearer (see direct orientation).

onset syllable: Prominent syllable that is the left edge boundary of the tonic segment and carries key choice.

phatic communication: Talk that is directed toward establishing good will between speakers rather than toward conveying information.

phonemic analysis: An approach to intonation analysis that proposes pitch and pause phonemes.

pitch: Our perception of whether a sound is high or low; created by the particular vibration of the vocal cords of the speaker.

pitch concord: Pitch range interactions between speakers in which a second speaker will aim to match their prosodic choices to those of the previous speaker; also called *prosodic alignment* or *prosodic matching* (see concord-breaking).

pitch level: See key.

pitch range: The range of a given speaker's voice.

pitch sequence: A stretch of consecutive tone units that fall between two low termination choices and are conceptually related; also called a pitch or speech paragraph.

positive affect: Creation of an environment in which participants feel positive feelings and emotions.

pragmatics: The study of the meaning and use of utterances within their situational context.

proclaiming tones: Fall and rise-fall tone choices.

prominence: Utterance or sentence-level stress.

prosodic composition: A collection of prosodic features that typically appear in particular language events and help to identify them.

prosodic mitigating device: A device used to mitigate the communicative message of the discourse such as the use of a level tone to mitigate disagreement.

prosodic repair: A speech repair undertaken by the speaker to correct prosodic information rather than some other kind of linguistic repair.

referring tones: Rise and fall-rise tone choices.

segmentals: Vowels and consonants.

semantic labeling: The tradition of labeling intonational patterns with particular attitudinal characteristics.

socially integrative function: A function of intonational choices to promote agreement or affiliation between speakers.

speaker normalization: A process by which hearers can estimate where a pitch appears in a given speaker's pitch range given enough context.

state of convergence: The continuous negotiation between speakers toward a roughly mutual state of understanding of the discourse that allows for successful communication; includes both informational and social convergence.

stress-timed: Traditional definition of a language's rhythmic properties in which the regular beats move from stressed syllable to stressed syllable.

stylized intonation: Intonation patterns often resulting from the "sing-song" patterns of nursery rhymes or verses.

suprasegmentals: Pitch, stress, volume, and pause patterns.

syllable timed: Traditional definition of a language's rhythmic properties in which stresses occur on each syllable at equal intervals in time.

teacher-induced error: Student errors that are the result of the classroom situation, such as the way a teacher uses teacher-talk or inadequate practice opportunities. Also called induced errors.

termination: Linguistically significant use of pitch level on the prominent tonic syllable divided into a three term system: High termination = particularizing function; Mid termination = additive function; Low termination = reformulating function or closing an interaction.

ToBI: A prosodic transcription system (Tones and Break Indices) originally used with the Autosegmental Metric approach.

tonal analysis: An approach to intonation within the British tradition that comprises a number of components, the most important of which is the nuclear or tonic syllable.

tone choice: Linguistically significant use of pitch movement on the prominent tonic syllable divided into: Falling tones (fall, rise-fall) that indicate new material; Rising tones (rise, fall-rise) that indicate known material, and a level tone (flat or with a slight rise) that indicates a neutral stance

tone units: Stretches of speech that form the pitch-defined units that comprise spoken discourse.

tonic segment: The meaning-bearing element of the tone unit comprising minimally of a tonic syllable.

tonic syllable: Prominent syllable that is the right edge boundary of the tonic segment and carries termination and tone choice.

Traditional Englishes: English varieties arising from the first diaspora such as U.S. or Australian Englishes.

uptalk: A manner of speaking in which declarative sentences are uttered with rising intonation at the end; also called *upspeak*.

REFERENCES

Abercrombie, D. (1967). *Elements of general phonetics*. Edinburgh: Edinburgh University Press.

Abu-Al-Makarem, A., & Petrosino, L. (2007). Reading and spontaneous speaking fundamental frequency of young Arabic men for Arabic and English languages: A comparative study. *Perceptual and Motor Skills, 105*(2), 572–580.

Anderson, L. (1990). Intonation, turn-taking and dysfluency: Non-natives conversing. In M. Hewings (Ed.), *Papers in discourse intonation* (pp. 102–113). Birmingham, England: University of Birmingham.

Arana, G. (2013). Creaky voice: Yet another example of young women's linguistic ingenuity. Retrieved from https://www.atlantic.com/sexes/archive/2013/01/creaky-voice-yet-another-example-of-young-womens-linguistic-ingenuity/267046

Armstrong, L. E., & Ward, I. C. (1926). *A handbook of English intonation*. Cambridge, England: Helfer.

Ashby, P., & Ashby, M. (1995). Spelling aloud: A preliminary study of idiomatic intonation. In J. Windsor Lewis (Ed.), *Studies in general and English phonetics* (pp. 145–154). London: Routledge.

Bailey, K. M. (1984). A typology of teaching assistants. In K. Bailey, F. Pialorsi, & J. Zukowski/Faust (Eds.), *Foreign teaching assistants in US universities* (pp. 110–125). Washington, DC: NAFSA.

Baker, A. (2011). Discourse prosody and teachers' stated beliefs and practices. *TESOL Journal, 2*(3), 263–292.

Barr, P. (1990). The role of discourse intonation in lecture comprehension. In M. Hewings (Ed.), *Papers in discourse intonation* (pp. 5–21). Birmingham, England: University of Birmingham.

Beckman, M. (1997). A typology of spontaneous speech. In Y. Sagisaka, N. Campbell, & N. Higuchi (Eds.), *Computing Prosody* (pp. 7–26). New York: Springer.

van Bezooijen, R. (1995). Sociocultural aspects of pitch differences between Japanese and Dutch women. *Language and Speech, 38*(3), 253–265.

Bloomfield, L. (1933). *Language*. New York: Henry Holt.

Bode, S. (1980). *Listening in & speaking out*. London: Longman.

Bolinger, D. L. (1951). Intonation: Levels versus configurations. *Word, 7*, 199–210.

Bolinger, D. L. (1961). Three analogies. *Hispania, 44*(1), 134–137.

Bolinger, D. (1986). *Intonation and its parts: Melody in spoken English*. Stanford, CA: Stanford University Press.

Bradford, B. (1988). *Intonation in context: Intonation practice for upper-intermediate and advanced learners of English, Teacher's book*. Cambridge, England: Cambridge University Press.

Brazil, D. (1985). *The communicative value of intonation in English*. Birmingham, England: University of Birmingham.

Brazil, D. (1997). *The communicative value of intonation in English*. Cambridge, England: Cambridge University Press. First published 1985, University of Birmingham.

Brazil, D., Coulthard, M., & Johns, C. (1980). *Discourse intonation and language teaching*. London: Longman.

Breiteneder, A., Pitzl, M., Majewski, S. & Klimpfinger. T. (2006). VOICE recording: Methodological challenges in the compilation of a corpus of spoken ELF. *Nordic Journal of English Studies,5*(2), 161–187. Special issue on ELF.

Burri, M. (2015). Student teachers' cognition about L2 pronunciation instruction: A case study. *Australian Journal of Teacher Education, 40*(10), 1–10.

Cauldwell, R. (2002). *Streaming speech: listening and pronunciation for advanced learners of English* (British/Irish ed.). Birmingham, England: Speech in Action.

Cauldwell, R. (2003). *Streaming speech*. Birmingham, England: Speech in Action.

Cauldwell, R. (2012). How friendly are the natives? An evaluation of native-speaker judgments of foreign-accented British and American English. *Journal of the International Phonetic Association, 42*(2), 213–215.

Cauldwell, R. (2013). *Phonology for listening*. Birmingham, England: Speech in Action.

Celce-Murcia, M., Brinton, D., & Goodwin, J. M. (1996). *Teaching pronunciation: A reference for teachers of English to speakers of other languages*. New York: Cambridge University Press.

Celce-Murcia, M., Brinton, D., Goodwin, J. & Griner, B. (2010). *Teaching Pronunciation* (2nd ed.). Cambridge, England: Cambridge University Press.

Chabot, J. (2006). *Sequences: Picture stories for ESL*. New York: Full Blast Productions.

Chela-Flores, B. (2008). Pronunciation and language learning: An integrative approach. *International Review of Applied Linguistics in Language Teaching, 39*(2), 85–101.

Cheng, W., Greaves, C., & Warren, M. (2008). *A corpus-driven study of discourse intonation: The Hong Kong corpus of spoken English (prosodic)*. Amsterdam: John Benjamins.

Chomsky, N. & Halle, M. (1968). *The sound pattern of English*. Cambridge : MIT Press.

Chun, D. M. (2002). *Discourse intonation in L2: From theory and research to practice*. Amsterdam: Benjamins.

Clennell, C. (1997). Raising the pedagogic status of discourse intonation teaching. *ELT Journal, 51*(2), 117–125.

Cogo, A., & Dewey, M. (2006). Efficiency in ELF communication: From pragmatic motives to lexico-grammatical innovation. *Nordic Journal of English Studies, 5*(2), 59–93.

Couper-Kuhlen, E. (1986). *An introduction to English prosody.* Tubingen, Germany: Max Niemeyer-Verlag.

Couper-Kuhlen, E. (1996). Towards an interactional perspective on prosody and a prosodic perspective on interaction. In E. Couper-Kuhlen & M. Selting (Eds.), *Prosody in conversation* (pp. 11–56). Cambridge, England: Cambridge University Press.

Couper-Kuhlen, E. (2001). Interactional prosody: High onsets in reason-for-the-call turns. *Language in Society, 30*(1), 29–53.

Couper-Kuhlen, E., & Selting, M. (1996). *Prosody in conversation: Interactional studies.* Cambridge, England: Cambridge University Press.

Cruttenden, A. (1997). *Intonation* (2nd ed.). Cambridge, England: Cambridge University Press.

Crystal, D. (1969). *Prosodic systems and intonation in English.* Cambridge, England: Cambridge University Press.

Crystal, D., & Davy, D. (1969). *Investigating English style.* Bloomington: Indiana University Press.

Cutler, A. (1983). Speakers' conceptions of the function of prosody. In A. Cutler & D. R. Ladd (Eds.), *Prosody: Models and measurements* (pp. 79–91). Berlin: Springer-Verlag.

Dauer, R. M. (1983). Stress-timing and syllable-timing reanalyzed. *Journal of Phonetics, 11*(1), 51–62.

Dauer, R. M. (2005). The lingua franca core: A new model for pronunciation instruction? *TESOL Quarterly, 39*(3), 543–550.

DeGaytan, C., & DeGaytan, M. (2012). Run for president. Demonstration session at 46th Annual TESOL Convention, Philadelphia.

Derwing, T., & Munro, M. (2005). Second language accent and pronunciation teaching: A research-based approach. *TESOL Quarterly, 39,* 379–397.

Derwing, T., Munro, M., & Wiebe, G. (1997). Pronunciation instruction for "fossilized" learners: Can it help? *Applied Language Learning, 8,* 217–235.

Derwing, T., Munro, M., & Wiebe, G. (1998). Evidence in favor of a broad framework for pronunciation instruction. *Language Learning, 48,* 393–410.

Deterding, D. (2005). Listening to estuary English in Singapore. *TESOL Quarterly, 39,* 425–440.

Deterding, D., & Kirkpatrick, A. (2006). Emerging South-East Asian Englishes and intelligibility. *World Englishes, 25,* 391–409.

Donato, R. (2004). Aspects of collaboration in pedagogical discourse. *Annual Review of Applied Linguistics, 24,* 284–302.

Donna, S. (2000). *Teaching business English.* New York: Cambridge University Press.

Drew, P., & Heritage, J. (1992). *Talk at work*. Cambridge, England: Cambridge University Press.

Duranti, A. (1986). The audience as co-author: An introduction. *Text & Talk, 6*(3), 239–247.

Eisenstein, M. (1983). Native reactions to non-native speech: A review of empirical research. *Studies in Second Language Acquisition, 5*(2), 160–176.

Evans, V. (2016). Beyond words: How language-like is emoji? Retrieved from https://blog.oup.com/2016/04/how-language-like-is-emoji

Foote, J. A., Holtby, A. K., & Derwing, T. M. (2012). Survey of the teaching of pronunciation in adult ESL programs in Canada, 2010. *TESL Canada Journal, 29*(1), 1–22.

Goffman, E. (1981). *Forms of talk*. Philadelphia: University of Pennsylvania Press.

Goh, C. (2000). A discourse approach to the description of intonation in Singapore English. In A. Brown, D. Deterding, & E. L. Low (Eds.), *The English language in Singapore: Research on pronunciation* (pp. 35–45). Singapore: Singapore Association for Applied Linguistics.

Goh, C. (2001). Discourse intonation of English in Malaysia and Singapore: Implications for wider communication and teaching. *RELC Journal, 32*(1), 92–105.

Gordon, J., & Darcy, I. (2016). The development of comprehensible speech in L2 learners. *Journal of Second Language Pronunciation, 2*(1), 56–92.

Gorsuch, G., Meyers, C. M., Pickering, L., & Griffee, D. T. (2010). *English communication for international teaching assistants*. Long Grove, IL: Waveland Press.

Gorsuch, G., Meyers, C. M., Pickering, L., & Griffee, D. T. (2013). *English communication for international teaching assistants* (2nd ed.). Long Grove, IL: Waveland Press.

Green, G. M. (1989). *Pragmatics and natural language understanding*. Mahwah, NJ: Lawrence Erlbaum Associates.

Gumperz, J. (1982). *Discourse strategies*. New York: Cambridge University Press.

Gumperz, J., & Hymes, D. (1972). *Directions in sociolinguistics: The ethnography of communication*. New York: Holt.

Gumperz, J., & Roberts, C. (1980). Developing awareness skills for interethnic communication. *Occasional Papers 12*. Singapore: SEAMEO Regional Language Center.

Gussenhoven, C. (1983). *A semantic analysis of the nuclear tones of English*. Bloomington: Indiana University Linguistics Club.

Halliday, M. A. K. (1967). *Intonation and grammar in British English*. The Hague: Mouton.

Halliday, M.A.K. (1970). *A course in spoken English*. Oxford, England: Oxford University Press.

Halliday, M. A. K., & Greaves, W. S. (2008). *Intonation in the grammar of English*. London: Equinox Publishing.

Hazel, S. (2016). Being a native speaker is globally useless if you can't speak other versions of English. Retrieved from https://qz.com/618702/

Hewings, M. (1995). Tone choice in the English intonation of non-native speakers. *The International Review of Applied Linguistics, 33*(3), 251–265.

Hewings, M., & Goldstein, S. (1998). *Pronunciation plus: Practice through interaction: North American English.* New York: Cambridge University Press.

Higgins, C. (2003). "Ownership" of English in the outer circle: An alternative to the NS-NNS dichotomy. *TESOL Quarterly,, 37*(4), 615–644.

Hincks, R. (2005). Measures and perceptions of liveliness in student oral presentation speech: A proposal for an automatic feedback mechanism. *System, 33*(4), 575–591.

Hinofotis, F., & Bailey, K. (1980). American undergraduates' reactions to the communication skills of foreign teaching assistants. *On TESOL, 80*, 120–133.

Hirst, D., & Di Cristo, A. (1998). *Intonation systems: A survey of twenty languages.* Cambridge, England: Cambridge University Press.

Honorof, D., & Whalen, D. (2005). Perception of pitch location within a speaker's F0 range. *Journal of the Acoustical Society of America, 117*(4), 2193–2200.

Jacoby, S., & Ochs, E. (1995). Co-construction: An introduction. *Research on Language and Social Interaction, 28*, 1–21.

Jassem, W., & Demnko, G. (1986). On extracting linguistic information from F0 traces. In C. Johns-Lewis (Ed.), *Intonation in discourse* (pp. 1–18). London: Croom Helm.

Jayaraj, J., Leelavathi, G., & Merlin, F. P. (2015). Reliability and impact of English in India: A historical overview. *International Journal Advances in Social Science and Humanities, 3*, 15–42.

Jenkins, J. (2009). *World Englishes: A resource book for students* (2nd ed.). London: Routledge.

Jenkins, J., Cogo, A., & Dewey, M. (2011). Review of developments in research into English as a lingua franca. *Language Teaching, 44*(3), 281–315.

Johns-Lewis, C. M. (1986). Prosodic differentiation of discourse modes. In C. Johns-Lewis (Ed.), *Intonation in discourse* (pp. 199–219). London: Croom Helm.

Kachru, B. B. (1985). The bilinguals' creativity. *Annual Review of Applied Linguistics, 6*, 20–33. Cambridge, England: Cambridge University Press.

Kandiah, T. (1998). Epiphanies of the deathless native user's manifold avatars: A postcolonial perspective on the native speaker. In R. Singh (Ed.), *The native speaker: Multilingual perspectives* (pp. 79–110). New Delhi, India: Sage Publications.

Kang, O., & Rubin, D. L. (2009). Reverse linguistic stereotyping: Measuring the effect of listener expectations on speech evaluation. *Journal of Language and Social Psychology, 28*(4), 441–456.

Kecskes, I. (2006). Formulaic language in ELF. In I. Kecskes & L. Horn (Eds.), *Explorations in pragmatics: Linguistic, cognitive & intercultural aspects* (pp. 2–28). New York: Mouton de Gruyter.

Kennedy, S., & Trofimovich, P. (2010). Language awareness and second language pronunciation: A classroom study. *Language Awareness, 19*, 171–185.

Koester, A. (1990). The intonation of agreeing and disagreeing in English and German. In M. Hewings (Ed.), *Papers in discourse intonation* (pp. 83–101). Birmingham, England: University of Birmingham.

Koshik, I. (2000). Conversation analytic research on institutional talk: Implications for TESOL teachers and researchers. *TESOL Research Interest Section Newsletter, 7*(2), 38–11.

Labov, W. (1972). *Sociolinguistic patterns.* Philadelphia: University of Pennsylvania Press.

Ladd, R. D. (1996). *Intonational phonology.* Cambridge, England: Cambridge University Press.

Lee, J., Jang, J., & Plonsky, L. (2015). The effectiveness of second language pronunciation instruction: A meta-analysis. *Applied Linguistics, 36*(3), 307–331.

Levelt, W. J. M. (1989). *Speaking: From intention to articulation.* Cambridge: MIT Press.

Levis, J. M. (2016). Research into practice: How research appears in pronunciation teaching materials. *Language Teaching, 49*(3), 423–437.

Levis, J., & Pickering, L. (2004). Teaching intonation in discourse using speech visualization technology. *System, 32*(4), 505–524.

Lippi-Green, R. (2012). *English with an accent* (2nd ed.). London: Routledge.

Levon, E. (2006). Hearing "gay": Prosody, interpretation, and the affective judgments of men's speech. *American Speech, 81*(1), 56–78.

Lieberman, P. (1966). *Intonation, perception, and language.* Cambridge: MIT Press.

Lomotey, C. F. (2015). *Intonation meaning in Ghanaian English discourse* (Unpublished dissertation). Texas A&M University–Commerce.

Macdonald, S. (2002). Pronunciation: Views and practices of reluctant teachers. *Prospect, 3*(17), 3–18.

Marks, J. (1999). Is stress-timing real? *English Language Teaching Journal, 53*(3), 191–199.

Mauranen, A. (2006). Signalling and preventing misunderstanding in ELF. *International Journal of the Sociology of Language, 177,* 123–150.

McKay, S. L. (2002). *Teaching English as an international language: Rethinking goals and perspectives.* New York: Oxford University Press.

McEwan, I. (2010). *Amsterdam.* New York: Anchor Books.

Menjo, S. (2016, August). *Using PEPS-C to investigate L2 prosodic acquisition of Japanese adult learners of English.* Paper presented at Pronunciation in Second Language Learning and Teaching Conference 2016, Calgary, Canada.

Mennen, I. (1999). The realisation of nucleus placement in second language intonation. *Proceedings of the 14th International Congress of Phonetic Sciences,* 555–558.

Mennen, I. (2007). Phonological and phonetic influences in non-native intonation. In J. Trouvain & U. Gut (Eds.), *Non-native prosody: Phonetic description & teaching practice* (pp. 53–76). Berlin: Mouton de Gruyter.

Meyers, C. (2014). Intelligible accented speakers as pronunciation models. In J. Levis & S. McCracklin (Eds.), *Proceedings of the 5th Annual Conference of Pronunciation in Second Language Learning and Teaching* (pp. 172–176). Ames: Iowa State University.

MICASE. (2000). History of the American family lecture (Transcript). (2000). Ann Arbor: University of Michigan English Language Institute.

Miller, S. (2000). *Targeting pronunciation.* Boston: Houghton Mifflin.

Mitrofanova, Y. (2012). Raising EFL students' awareness of English intonation functioning. *Language Awareness, 21*(3), 279–291.

Motormouth interrupt. (n.d.).Retrieved from http://changingminds.org/techniques/conversation/interrupting/motormouth_interrupt.htm

Müller, F. E. (1996). Affiliating and disaffiliating with continuers: Prosodic aspects of recipiency. In E. Couper-Kuhlen & M. Selting (Eds.), *Prosody in conversation* (pp. 131–176). New York: Cambridge University Press.

Murphy, J. (2014). Myth 7: Teacher training programs provide adequate preparation in how to teach pronunciation. In L. Grant (Ed.), *Pronunciation myths: Applying second language research to classroom teaching* (pp. 188–234). Ann Arbor: University of Michigan Press.

Myers, S., Zhong, M., & Guan, S. (1998). Instructor immediacy in the Chinese college classroom. *Communication Studies, 49*(3), 240–254.

Nazzi, T., & Ramus, F. (2003). Perception and acquisition of linguistic rhythm by infants. *Speech Communication, 41,* 233–243.

Nelson, C. L. (1985). My language, your culture: Whose communicative competence? *World Englishes, 4*(2), 243–250.

Nelson, C. L. (1995). Intelligibility and world Englishes in the classroom. *World Englishes, 14*(2), 273–279.

Nordquist, R. (n.d.). Punctuation matters: A "Dear John" letter and a two million dollar comma. Retrieved from www.infoplease.com/language-arts/grammar-and-spelling/punctuation-punctuation-matters

Obama, B. (2006, November 13). *Martin Luther King Jr. national memorial groundbreaking ceremony.* Retrieved from http://obamaspeeches.com/093-Martin-Luther-King-Memorial-Groundbreaking-Ceremony-Obama-Speech.htm

O'Brien, M. G. (2014). L2 learners' assessments of accentedness, fluency, and comprehensibility of native and nonnative German speech. *Language Learning, 64*(4), 715–748.

O'Connor, J.D. (1980). *Better English pronunciation.* Cambridge, England: Cambridge University Press.

O'Connor, J. D., & Arnold, G. F. (1961). *Intonation of colloquial English* (2nd ed.). London: Longman.

Ohala, J. J., & Gilbert, J. B. (1981). Listeners' ability to identify languages by their prosody. In P. Léon & M. Rossi (Eds.), *Problèmes de prosodie Vol. II: Expérimentations, modèles et fonctions* (pp. 123–131). Ottawa: Didier.

Ouafeu, T. S. Y. (2010). *Intonational meaning in Cameroon English discourse: A sociolinguistic perspective.* Newcastle, England: Cambridge Scholars.

Palmer, H. E. (1922). *English intonation with systematic exercises.* Cambridge, England: W. Heffer & Sons.

Pandey, P. K. (1981). On a description of the phonology of Indian English. *Central Institute of English and Foreign Languages Bulletin, 17*(1), 11–19.

Pandit, N. (1979). Caste and class in Maharashtra. *Economic and Political Weekly*, 425–436.

Park, H. (2016). It is "broken" and "accented": Non-native English-speaking (NNES) graduate students' perceptions toward NNES instructors' English. From http://docs.lib.purdue.edu/open_access_dissertations/826.

Pickering, L. (1999). *The analysis of prosodic systems in the classroom discourse of native speaker and nonnative speaker teaching assistants* (Unpublished doctoral dissertation). University of Florida, Gainesville.

Pickering, L. (2001). The role of tone choice in improving ITA communication in the classroom. *TESOL Quarterly, 35*, 233–255.

Pickering, L. (2004). The structure and function of intonational paragraphs in native and non-native instructional discourse. *English for Specific Purposes, 23*, 19–43.

Pickering, L. (2009). Intonation as a pragmatic resource in ELF interaction. *Intercultural Pragmatics, 6*(2), 235–255.

Pickering, L., & Levis, J. (2002, April). *Assessing the intonation patterns of second language learners.* Presented at the 36th Annual TESOL Convention, Salt Lake City, UT.

Pickering, L., & Litzenberg, J. (2011). Intonation as a pragmatic resource, revisited. In A. Archibald, A. Cogo & J. Jenkins (Eds). *Latest trends in ELF* (pp. 77–92). Newcastle, England: Cambridge Scholars.

Pickering, L., & Wiltshire, C. (2000). Pitch accent in Indian English TA's teaching discourse. *World Englishes, 19*, 173–183.

Pierrehumbert, J. (1980). *The phonology and phonetics of English intonation.* Bloomington: Indiana University Linguistics Club.

Pierrehumbert, J., & Hirschberg, J. (1990). The meaning of intonational contours in the interpretation of discourse. In P. R. Cohen, J. Morgan, & M. E. Pollack (Eds.), *Intentions in communication* (pp. 271–311). Cambridge: MIT Press.

Pike, K. L. (1945). *The intonation of American English.* Ann Arbor: University of Michigan.

Pirt, G. (1990). Discourse intonation problems for non-native speakers. In M. E. Hewings (Ed.), *Papers in discourse intonation* (pp. 145–155). Birmingham, England: University of Birmingham.

Pitzl, M. (2005). Non-understanding in English as a lingua franca: Examples from a business context. *Vienna English Working Papers, 14*(2), 50–71. Retrieved from http://www.univie.ac.at/Anglistik/Views0502mlp.pdf

Platt, J. T., & Ho, M. L. (1989). Discourse particles in Singaporean English: Substratum influences and universals. *World Englishes, 8*(2), 215–221.

Princess Diana. (1993, June 1). *Speech on women and mental health.* Retrieved from https://www.youtube.com/watch?=cZFvJg28czs.

Ramírez Verdugo, D. (2006). A study of intonation awareness and learning in nonnative speakers of English. *Language Awareness, 15*(3), 141–159.

Ramus, F., & Mehler, J. (1999). Language identification with suprasegmental cues: A study based on speech resynthesis. *Journal of the Acoustical Society of America, 105*(1), 512–521.

Reed, M., & Michaud, C. (2015). Intonation in research and practice: The importance of metacognition. In M. Reed & J. Levis (Eds.), *The handbook of English pronunciation* (pp. 454–470). West Sussex, England: John Wiley & Sons.

Reisman, K. (1974). Contrapuntal conversations in an Antiguan village. In R. Bauman & J. Sherzer (Eds.), *Explorations in the ethnography of speaking* (pp. 110–124). London: Cambridge University Press.

Richmond, K. C. (1984). *Teacher-induced errors.* Paper presented at the Annual Meeting of the California Association of Teachers of English to Speakers of Other Languages, San Jose, CA.

Roberts, C., & Campbell, S. (2006). *Talk on trial: Job interviews, language and ethnicity* (No. 344). Corporate Document Services.

Robins, R. H. (1967). *A short history of linguistics.* London: Longman.

Rubin, D. (2011). *The power of prejudice in accent perception: Reverse linguistic stereotyping and its impact on listener judgments and decisions.* Paper presented at the 3rd Pronunciation in Second Language Learning and Teaching Conference, Ames, IA.

Sacks, H., Schlegloff, E., & Jefferson, G. (1974). A simplest systematics for the organization of turn-taking in conversation. *Language,* (50), 696–735.

Sahgal, A. (1991). Patterns of language use in a bilingual setting in India. In R. K. Agnihotri & A. L. Khanna (Eds.), *Second language acquisition: Socio-cultural and linguistic aspects of English in India* (pp. 265–273). Thousand Oaks, CA: Sage Publications, Inc.

Saito, K. (2012). Effects of instruction on L2 pronunciation development: A synthesis of 15 quasi-experimental intervention studies. *TESOL Quarterly, 46*(4), 842–854.

Saito, Y., & Saito, K. (2016). Differential effects of instruction on the development of second language comprehensibility, word stress, rhythm, and intonation: The case of inexperienced Japanese EFL learners. *Language Teaching Research, 21*(5), 589–608.

Sapir, E. (1921). *Language: An introduction to the study of speech.* New York: Harcourt.

Schiffrin, D. (1994). *Approaches to discourse.* Oxford, England: Blackwell.

Seidlhofer, B. (2013). *Understanding English as a lingua franca.* Oxford, England: Oxford University Press.

Simpson, R. C., Briggs, S. L., Ovens, J., & Swales, J. M. (2002). *The Michigan corpus of academic spoken English.* Ann Arbor: University of Michigan English Language Institute.

Speakingout. (n.d.). Retrieved from http://www.princessdianaforever.com/speakingout.

Sridhar, K. (1997). The languages of India in New York. In O. García & J. A. Fishman (Eds.), *The multilingual apple: Languages in New York City.* Berlin: Walter de Gruyter.

Staples, S. (2014). *Linguistic characteristics of international and U.S. nurse discourse* (Unpublished doctoral dissertation). Northern Arizona University, Flagstaff, AZ.

Steele, J. (1775). *An essay towards establishing the melody and measure of speech to be expressed and perpetuated by peculiar symbols.* London: T. Payne and Son.

Stenson, N. (1983). Induced errors. In B. W. Robinett & J. Schachter (Eds.), *Second language learning: Contrastive analysis, error analysis and related aspects* (pp. 256–271). Ann Arbor: University of Michigan Press.

Stockwell, R. P. (1964). *Realism in historical English phonology.* Paper presented at the winter meeting of the Linguistics Society of America, University of California, Los Angeles.

Sweet, H. (1890). *A primer of spoken English.* Oxford, England: Clarendon Press.

Szczepek Reed, B. (2006). *Prosodic orientation in English conversation.* New York: Palgrave Macmillan.

Tannen, D. (1981). The machine-gun question: An example of conversational style. *Journal of Pragmatics, 5,* 383–397.

Tench, P. (1996). *The intonation systems of English.* London: Cassell.

Thomson, R., & Derwing, T. (2015). The effectiveness of L2 pronunciation instruction: A narrative review. *Applied Linguistics, 36,* 326–344.

Trouvain, J., & Gut, U. (2007). *Non-native prosody: Phonetic description and teaching practice.* Berlin: Mouton de Gruyter.

Tyler, A., & Davies, C. (1990). Cross-linguistic communication missteps. *Text-Interdisciplinary Journal for the Study of Discourse, 10*(4), 385–412.

Walker, R. (2010). *Teaching the pronunciation of English as a lingua franca.* Oxford, England: Oxford University Press.

Wennerstrom, A. (1994). Intonational meaning in English discourse: A study of nonnative speakers. *Applied Linguistics, 15*(4), 399–420.

Wennerstrom, A. K. (1997). *Discourse intonation and second language acquisition: Three genre-based studies* (Unpublished doctoral dissertation). University of Washington, Seattle.

Wennerstrom, A. K. (2001). *The music of everyday speech: Prosody and discourse analysis.* New York: Oxford University Press.

Wichmann, A. (2000). *Intonation in text and discourse: Beginnings, middles, and ends.* Harlow, England: Pearson Education Limited.

Wong, P., & Diehl, R. (2003). Perceptual normalization for inter- and intratalker variation in Cantonese level tones. *Journal of Speech Language and Hearing Research, 46,* 413–421.

Wrembel, M. (2007). Metacompetence-based approach to the teaching of L2 prosody: Practical implications. In U. G. Jürgen Trouvain (Ed.), *Non-native prosody: Phonetic description and teaching practice* (pp. 189–210). Berlin: Mouton de Gruyter.

Yates, L., & Zielinski, B. (2009). *Give it a go: Teaching pronunciation to adults.* Sydney: AMEP Research Centre.

Yule, G. (1980). Speakers' topics and major paratones. *Lingua, 52,* 33–47.

Zielinski, B., & Yates, L. (2014). Myth 3: Pronunciation instruction is not appropriate for beginner-level learners. In L. Grant (Ed.), *Pronunciation myths: Applying second language research to classroom teaching* (pp. 56–79). Ann Arbor: University of Michigan Press.

Index